Talismans
and Tarot

Magical Tools to Amplify, Attract & Manifest

LORI LYTLE

FOREWORD BY Benebell Wen

WEISER BOOKS

This edition first published in 2025 by Weiser Books, an imprint of
Red Wheel/Weiser, LLC
With offices at:
65 Parker Street, Suite 7
Newburyport, MA 01950
www.redwheelweiser.com

ISBN: 978-1-57863-875-8

Library of Congress Cataloging-in-Publication Data available upon request.

Cover design by Sky Peck Design
Interior by Michele Quinn
Interior images from *The Weiser Tarot* © Red Wheel/Weiser. All rights
     reserved
Typeset in Warnock Pro

Printed in the United States of America
IBI
10 9 8 7 6 5 4 3 2 1

FSC   FSC® C183721
MIX
Paper

For Rachel Pollack,
who said something to me that changed my life.

For my Matthew, who makes me feel magical.

Contents

Foreword

My first talisman was a divinity card my mother tucked into my school back-pack. "To help you do well in school," she said. One side of the card featured a painting of Kuan Yin and on the other, indecipherable sigils and calligraphy blessed by a nun. When I lost that divinity card, I panicked, but Mom said don't worry, it just means the talisman has completed its purpose. I graduated sixth grade in one piece, so guess that validates the magic.

Thinking back, that my first talisman was a divinity card somewhat reminiscent of tarot seems like kismet. Many of us have similar accounts of lucky pennies, pendants, charms, and stones we cling to for luck and protection, all while assuring others and ourselves that we follow evidence-based science. This isn't the contradiction that we think it is—science explains the material world while mystical practices address emotional and spiritual needs that science cannot fulfill. A tactile focal point like the familiar iconography on a tarot card can help us to adapt, to navigate, and to be resilient when faced with challenging times. Tarot divination is a form of mindfulness practice. Holding an acorn, or a cimaruta pendant can give us a sense of control, which then empowers us to seize control of our circumstances and effect change. Engaging with symbolic systems like tarot and ritual expands our creative thinking abilities and supports cognitive function.

In *Talismans and Tarot*, Lori explains the role of ritual and archetypal symbolism, how talismans become imbued with personal meaning through their association with our heritage, ancestry, and of cultural or religious values that are important to us. Talismans and amulets activate our inner reservoir of psychic energy. It's as psychological as it is magical. We're the ones channeling and directing our own inner resources to achieve a stated goal.

"Tarot cards are magic in tangible form," writes Lytle. You form a bond with the deck just as you do with a talisman, empowering a symbolic system to operate as a talisman. Like hieroglyphs (the word itself a Greek translation of the Egyptian phrase "the god's words"), the talismanic art of the tarot is itself a divine language. The symbols of the tarot activate something within us, an inner knowing at the unconscious level, and through ritual, we integrate those energies into conscious awareness. The drawing and dealing of cards become a magical incantation.

Both talismans and tarot are symbolic containers, which in Jungian psychology are physical objects that hold and represent mental energy. The tarot presents universal archetypal patterns—ways to cultivate a more fulfilling human experience. A talisman is a containment that empowers us and when that talisman is a tarot card imbued with the powers of history and consensus reality, it amplifies your magic.

This book will guide you on how to combine the sacred wisdom of tarot with the tangible power of talismans, and access something that our ancestors understood innately, which is that transformation requires both vision and vessel. As you turn these pages, you'll discover that this isn't just another book about tarot or magical objects. It's an invitation to weave together two profound traditions in a way that makes both more powerful. It's a practical guide to creating lasting change, yes, but it's also something rarer: a reminder that magic doesn't require us to abandon reason, but rather to expand upon it. *Talismans and Tarot* shows us that sometimes the most powerful magic comes from combining traditions in new ways.

In an age where we're often told to dismiss anything we cannot immediately explain, there's something rebellious—and deeply necessary—about reclaiming these practices and mystical traditions, and asserting boldly that magic exists in the space between what we can explain and what we can only experience. Let this book be your guide into that space. Let Lori show you how to bridge the momentary insight of a tarot reading with the sustained power of a talisman. Most importantly, let these chapters remind you that magic isn't something that happens to us—it's something we do.

Today, we are still exploring that bridge between ancient folk and modern scientific understanding of magical intention-setting. Personally, I do not know how an engine works, but I still drive my car from Point A to Point B, and I cannot explain the intricate science of most modern tools we rely on today, yet I use them intuitively, simply trusting that they work. Likewise, how talismans, tarot, and intention-setting through ritual can so powerfully create positive change and protection in my life eludes me, yet these practices have enriched my spirituality and helped me to advance my personal growth.

Lori and I have known each other for years through the tarot community, connecting as colleagues at various conferences and sharing insights in this unique space. What I think you, dear reader, should know about Lori is that she is by nature a mystic, and one who exudes positivity and kindness. From her aura you can discern that she has a deep connection to divinity, that Goddess speaks through her. Lori's embodiment of the priestess is both inspiring and palpable. *Talismans and Tarot*, and truly all that she offers the world of tarot, demonstrates her breadth and depth of knowledge of cartomancy combined with her natural abilities as a teacher. She is truly a luminary in this field and perfectly positioned to be guiding us on this journey as we study the interplay of talismans and tarot.

Benebell Wen
author of *Holistic Tarot*

Introduction: Making Magic

This book combines three of my favorite things—tarot, magic, and jewelry. I love shiny things. I love crystals and gemstones and jewelry. I always have. It runs in my DNA, particularly from my mother's side. But for the most part, I don't wear jewelry just because it's pretty (not that there's anything wrong with that). For me, it must have a meaning, a purpose, or a personal association. Putting on jewelry is a daily ritual and a devotional activity, and the pieces I choose become talismans that help me amplify my energy and manifest my intention.

Without really understanding the significance of it, I started working with amulets, lucky charms, and talismans as a kid. Throughout my childhood, I wore a guardian angel pendant that my Oma gave me and, over time, I added an Evil Eye and other protective charms. My pockets were always filled with crystals, small figurines, foreign coins, and other fascinating found objects that brought me luck. It's still the same today; my purse is always really heavy.

The words "amulet" and "talisman" may sound archaic or old-fashioned to some—superstitious objects that our ancestors believed in that have no widespread relevance now. But I am convinced that this is not the case. People today still put their faith in lucky charms. We have lucky pieces of clothing that we wear until they fall apart. We adorn ourselves with symbolic images and trust in amulets for protection. We carry talismans we hope will improve our lives and help us reach our goals. Humans have always turned to these touchstones when fearful or in need of comfort, or when inspired and ambitious and wanting to believe that anything is possible in this life.

Lucky charms will always have their place in my heart and in my pockets. But for years now, I've been focusing on working with talismans. A talisman is a magical tool—usually a piece of jewelry or something small enough to fit in your pocket—that supports you in manifesting an intention, a goal, or a desire.

Once you charge it with your energy and consecrate it with a ritual, a talisman amplifies your power and draws opportunities to you.

I also love the tarot. The cards inspire me, and I weave magic with them as well. And that's why I wrote this book. After many years of personal practice, I became aware that I'd been using talismans and tarot separately, but with the same intention—to help me manifest my goals and move confidently toward my hopes and dreams. Revelation! And that's the idea that this book explores. In it, I show you how you can combine talismans and tarot to dream big, work your unique magic, and manifest your desires.

The book is divided into two parts. In Part I, you'll learn about the foundations of magical work. We'll talk about talismans, what they are, and why they are powerful tools for manifesting magic. Then, because it can be used as an essential tool for creating talismans, we'll explore the tarot—what it is, what the cards can do for you, and how to read a tarot spread. Here you'll find interpretations for all the cards, as well as affirmations, and musings designed to spark reflection, curiosity, and discovery.

In Part II, you'll learn how to create a talisman. We'll discuss how to set an intention—the goal you want to manifest—which is the reason for crafting a talisman in the first place. We'll examine different materials you can use to ensure that you choose the most potent and meaningful talisman for you. I'll give you a specially designed tarot spread that can help you get laser-sharp clarity on what you want to manifest and how you will do that. Then you'll learn how to create and perform a consecration ritual that brings all these elements together and turns a mundane object into a magical tool. Finally, I'll show you how to work with your talisman to manifest your intention and achieve your desired change with certainty, flow, and joy.

I suggest that you start from the beginning of the book and work your way through the exercises, meditations, tarot readings, and musings you find along the way. Each chapter builds on the previous one, but I think you'll find that you are weaving magic from the moment you start. You can refer back to chapters 3 and 4—which include descriptions and interpretations of the tarot cards—as you move forward. They are intended to support you and help you create your own connections and personal meanings.

To use this book, all you need is a tarot deck, a talisman, and—most important—your curiosity and force of will. Your success depends on your compassionate heart and a belief in your power to manifest your dreams. Any tarot deck will do. Choose one that you love and that you enjoy working with. The card interpretations I give here are based on the Waite-Smith tradition, and the card images are those that adorn the beautiful Weiser Tarot. I recommend that you keep a journal in which you record your experiences, thoughts, and impressions as you work through the steps to create and use your talisman. The musings found throughout the book are prompts for reflection—internally or in your journal—to help guide you in this practice.

You likely picked up this book because you have a goal or dream that you're ready to manifest. You may have received just a hint or a whisper, or you may already have a crystal-clear intention in mind. That's so exciting! Give yourself a moment right now to imagine how you will feel and what your life will be like once you manifest your desire. Take a deep breath and connect with the power and magic within you. Trust in your ability to create positive change.

By the end of this book, you will have created a one-of-a-kind magical talisman with the support of the Tarot. Your talisman will amplify your focus and guide you toward manifesting your desire with clarity, trust, and, ultimately, success.

Ready? Let's start making some magic!

PART ONE

The Basics

CHAPTER 1

What Is a Talisman?

L et's start at the beginning—what a talisman is, what it is not, and what it can do for you. The short answer is that a talisman is a magical tool, usually a piece of jewelry you can wear or something small enough to tuck in your pocket, that supports you in manifesting a specific intention, goal, or desire.

A talisman starts out as an ordinary object—perhaps a crystal or a silver charm. Each will have its own unique structure, size, color, vibration, and energetic properties. You may appreciate this object for its beauty, or you may be interested in its characteristics. But you have no spiritual connection to it until you infuse it with your intention, your will, and your energy. When you create a bond between yourself and this object, you transform it into a magical tool and agree to work with it toward a shared and marvelous purpose.

For thousands of years, humans have created and used magical tools like amulets, talismans, and lucky charms. These tactile, material objects allow us to focus our energy. They become containers for our wishes and intentions. They provide a comforting presence in our pockets, on our fingers, or around our necks when we are uncertain, afraid, or hopeful. Although people often use these terms interchangeably, there are essential differences in how amulets, talismans, and lucky charms operate and what they can do for you. And it's important to be aware of those differences.

Amulets are passive protectors; talismans are active manifesters; lucky charms fall somewhere in between. Amulets and lucky charms counteract fear of the unknown or fear of vulnerability in the world. They help you control the forces around you. Talismans facilitate positive change and help you achieve a desired result, rather than avoiding something unwanted.

Let's first take a closer look at examples of traditional amulets and lucky charms. Then we'll explore why, although all these magical tools are valuable and helpful, talismans are the most powerful choice for your magical work.

AMULETS

Amulets protect. They shield against any danger or misfortune you may encounter and ward off unwanted energy directed at you. Rather than drawing your desire to you, amulets react to threats.

Amulets empower a form of *apotropaic* magic, a term that derives from the Greek word meaning "to turn away." The term is used to describe protective tools like amulets, as well as gestures like knocking on wood, crossing your fingers, making the sign of the horns, or the *manu fica*, a sign used to ward off evil spirits. Examples of apotropaic devices have appeared in architectural features and sculpture throughout history, and you can still find them today. Wonderfully grotesque and frightening faces, like those of gargoyles and gorgons, are painted or carved in stone and placed in vulnerable places like doorways, windows, fireplaces, and other entrances to buildings. As with amulets, their task is to protect the occupants and keep the structure safe from fire, flood, and other disasters.

Like a talisman, an amulet is usually a small object that you keep close to you so that it can work its protective magic. You may wear a trusted amulet every day or decide to put one on when heading into a daunting or risky situation. Perhaps you wear a guardian angel charm that a loved one gave you, or a pentacle or ankh pendant that uplifts your spirit. Or perhaps you carry a smooth pebble in your pocket that you found on the beach. These objects can be made of natural materials, or handcrafted, or manufactured. What matters most is your connection to them and your faith in their power.

And where does that power come from? There are many opinions on the answer to this question. But at the heart of them all is the belief that amulets connect with a higher power—the Divine or a particular deity, the universe, nature, ancestors, spirit guides, or your higher self. However you see them, amulets are reminders that there are forces around you that have your back.

Below are three examples of amulets that can give you an idea of their characteristics.

The Evil Eye

We've all felt the power of a look—an angry glare, a flash of envy, or a gaze of admiration—whether it's aimed at us or emanating from us. So it's no wonder that amulets that protect against the Evil Eye are some of the most common, recognizable, and treasured. Belief in the Evil Eye has been around for thousands of years. There are references to it in Sumerian and Babylonian cuneiform clay tablets that date back as far as 3000 BCE, and you can still find examples of it across cultures and countries today.

The Evil Eye is grounded in the belief that others can send harm your way with a look, and that those sending that energy are doing so maliciously or unaware of the illness, loss, and adversity they are causing. Amulets that ward off the Evil Eye most commonly take the shape of an eye—usually a blue eye. Often, they are made of blue glass and mimick the human eye, with concentric circles of dark blue, white, light blue, and black. They also sometimes appear as simple blue glass beads or as the *hamsa* hand, a universal sign of protection, power, and strength that dates back to ancient Mesopotamia.

I discovered this symbol while living in Greece and studying archeology. Evil Eyes were everywhere, peering unblinking from every window, rearview mirror, shop, wrist, or necklace. The ancient Greeks painted apotropaic eyes on terracotta wine cups to protect from evil while drinking, and on ships' bows to keep them on course and clear of harm.

And this archaic practice survives today. I wear an amulet to repel the Evil Eye almost every day. I sometimes wear two bracelets made of blue glass beads, one on each wrist, to create a circuit of protective energy. If I'm going to be in a crowded place charged with anxiety, frustration, or excitement—like an airport or a big event—I deck myself out with multiple eyes. It's satisfying to know that my amulets are quietly doing their job of scanning and shielding against harm, so I can focus on other things. When an Evil Eye pendant or bracelet cracks or falls off the chain, you know it has protected you well.

Cimaruta

The cimaruta is an Italian folk amulet that is also referred to as a "witch's charm." It appears most often as a silver pendant in the shape of a sprig of rue, with its characteristic three branches. According to folklore, rue defends against malicious magic, sinister forces, and envy. Protective and lucky symbols were often hung on rue branches, adding to the cimaruta's potency. Although the symbols vary over time and region, some of the most common are hands, flowers, keys, crescent moons, hearts, horns, and animals (roosters, snakes, and frogs in particular).

Although some believe that the function of a cimaruta is to protect the wearer from witchcraft and witches, this is not the case. Although they ward off harmful magic, that doesn't equate to witchcraft, since witches are also interested in warding off dark enchantments. Cimarutas are dripping with symbols beloved to witches, adorned with signs associated with the goddesses Diana and Artemis, as well as images that honor the powers of nature. I wear a cimaruta to show love and reverence for the Goddess, as well as for the aura of protection it creates.

Acorn

An acorn is an example of a natural amulet. Mighty oak trees come from humble acorns, representing long life, strength, and potential. Carrying an acorn protects you from illness, prevents aging, and keeps you full of vigor.

The Norse god Thor is fond of acorns, and placing one on your windowsill protects your home from lightning. After a lightning storm in my neighborhood, I put an acorn on the windowsills in each corner of my house and, knock on wood, they keep me on Thor's good side.

MUSINGS

- Do you wear or carry an amulet? If so, how did it come into your possession?

- Do you wear it daily or only under exceptional circumstances?

- If you no longer have it, what happened to it?

∞∞

LUCKY CHARMS

Lucky charms fall somewhere in between amulets and talismans. Like amulets, they protect while attracting good fortune. But they're not ritually consecrated like talismans and don't have a specific purpose beyond good luck. Rather than just reacting to threats, they call in opportunities and synchronicities. A lucky charm can be anything that has meaning for you. It's especially promising if you find one unexpectedly. That's a sign of a lucky day or an opportunity not to be missed.

Your own belief powers lucky charms. Whether your confidence in their power comes from long-held traditions or cultural significance or superstition, most of us agree that certain objects bring luck. That belief is most potent when you have a personal connection with a charm and trust it because you've seen it work for you in the past. This gives you faith it will work again. For instance, many students have particular pens or pencils that they swear have brought them good results, so they use them for every exam.

Many people have personal lucky charms—a T-shirt they've worn until it's ready to fall apart, a hat with their favorite team's logo, a beloved piece of heirloom jewelry, a childhood toy, or a found object that appeared just when they needed luck. Traditional and beloved examples of lucky charms are pennies, horseshoes, and four-leaf clovers.

Lucky Pennies

Pennies are only lucky when you happen to find one. Finding a penny is a sign that you've been singled out for good fortune, and that the gods are smiling on you. And beware! You tempt fate if you don't pick it up. If you pass up good luck, it may not return.

Some say that finding a penny heads up or from the year of your birth is especially fortunate. Some believe that repeating a spoken rhyme or song can enhance the power of this charm. When I was a kid, whenever we spotted a penny on the ground, we said: "Find a penny, pick it up, and all day long, you'll have good luck." And we did.

Horseshoes

Horseshoes are believed to bring good luck and protection. They are made of iron, a metal known to ward off evil spirits, and have seven nail holes, a lucky number. They are traditionally hung over a doorway to protect the space within.

But the big question is whether you should you hang a horseshoe with its ends pointing up or down. Folklore tells us that a horseshoe catches and collects good luck when pointing up. When pointing down, luck spills out and is shared with anyone who passes beneath it.

Four-Leaf Clovers

Finding a four-leaf clover is a thrilling and rare event. In fact, four-leaf clovers are said to be lucky precisely *because* of their rarity. When you find one, you know it is an extraordinary occurrence, and that perhaps the fates or the fairies are sending you a gift. Some stories claim that finding a four-leaf clover gives you the power to see fairies and to ward off malevolent spirits. Another recounts that Eve plucked a four-leaf clover in the Garden of Eden and took it with her when she was cast out as a reminder of her time in Paradise. The four leaves came to represent faith, hope, luck, and love.

Four-leaf clovers have a special significance for me. One summer, when my family was going through the loss of a loved one, I found at least one four-leaf clover every day, sometimes more. Those persistent clovers reminded me that there is still magic in the world, even at the worst of times. I kept them and pressed them in the pages of my hardcover cookbooks. Now, when one falls out unexpectedly, it always makes me smile. You can't force the sighting of a four-leaf clover; they show themselves to you when you need them.

◇◇

MUSINGS

- Do you wear or carry a lucky charm? If so, how did it come into your possession?

- Do you wear it daily or only under exceptional circumstances?

- If you no longer have it, what happened to it?

◇◇

TALISMANS

Now let's bring our focus back to talismans. As we have seen, these are magical tools that are usually something small enough to carry or wear. They can be made of any material. Their purpose is to help you manifest a specific desire. That is why you create one. And that's a crucial point. You must *create* your talisman. To transform it into your magical ally, you must charge it with your intention and energy, and form a connection with it through a consecration ritual so that it can amplify your power and draw advantageous opportunities to you.

I often teach workshops on how to create and use talismans. Although you will choose your own talisman material, I select objects everyone can work with at these workshops for logistical reasons. I then guide the participants through the steps of the creation and consecration process, but they do their own magical work.

Among my favorite talismans to work with at workshops are large old-fashioned keys hung on cords as pendants. Some keys are plain; some are decorated with symbols and inscriptions; others are shaped like animals or mythical creatures. I lay piles of keys on a table at the front of the room and invite everyone to choose one. I love watching as people make their choices. Some choose quickly, while others hunt carefully through them until they find the right one.

Workshop attendees know they will be creating a talisman to support them in achieving an intention or a goal, so they are already working magic when they select their talisman, no matter how they do it. A heart-shaped key may indicate an intention of attracting love or achieving a heart's desire. A crescent moon suggests divination, connecting with the Goddess, or tapping into primal instincts. A key shaped like a seahorse hints at the ability to go into deep waters and always bob back to the surface.

And why do I choose keys? Well, keys lock and unlock. They unlock doors, boxes, hearts, and books, and open the way to knowledge and opportunities. But a key can also lock an intention in your heart and mind, or lock away something you want to keep safe but still want to access. A key puts you in control of opening and closing, revealing and concealing.

You will also choose the day for creating your own talisman, but at these workshops, the day is chosen for us. So we tap into that day's inherent energy. For example, Sunday is sacred to the sun, calling on energies that facilitate growth, success, and joy; International Women's Day is a day of empowerment, equality, and positive change; at Daylight Savings, we spring forward; the day before a Full Moon suggests culmination and illumination. In the workshops, we make the most of these contributing factors.

When you create your own talisman, you will have many factors to consider, including your intention, the material you choose, when you do your work and how you prepare for it, the tarot reading you draw, and the consecration ritual you use. All of these factors will affect how you work with your talisman. Within this framework, however, you will have the flexibility to create a magical tool that is perfect for you. You don't have to stick to tradition or follow any rules. You can be as creative, as playful, as serious, or as somber as you like. You're going to do something that's never been done before and won't be done again, because it reflects who you are and where you are in this moment. Your talisman will be precisely what it needs to be.

Before we go any deeper into this process, however, it's crucial that you understand where a talisman's power comes from. Key factors in that power are intention, physicality, ritual, and sympathetic forces. Let's take a brief look at each one before moving on to the next chapter.

Intention

Your intention is the reason you create a talisman in the first place. You have a need or a desire, or a change that you intend to manifest using magic to support your effort and will. So it only makes sense that your magic will be more potent, and the results more satisfying when your intention is crystal clear. After all, how can you manifest what you want if you're unsure of what that is?

When you create a talisman, you put your intention out into the world. You say: "I'm committed to manifesting this intention, and I know I can do it." In a sense, you've *already* created your desired outcome on the energetic level. But you still have to do the work. Your talisman boosts your energy and confidence, and brings circumstances into greater alignment with your purpose, but it's up to you to act. Taking action toward your goal shows your force of will and builds momentum; wishing and waiting aren't enough. Combined with the magic you work, your talisman's inherent properties boost your power and energy, and spur you on to action.

Physicality

A talisman is a physical reminder of your intention—a tangible focus for your will and desire. When you wear it, or admire its beauty, or feel its weight in your hand, it brings your intention to the forefront of your heart and mind. It carries your feelings about your intention; it embodies your hopes; it represents how you imagine your life will improve when you've achieved your goal. The material you choose for your talisman is essential, but the fact that it is a solid object that engages your senses is already powerful.

Ritual

Although there are several steps to creating a talisman, the ritual that consecrates it is the crucial element that brings everything together and transforms a crystal, or a pendant, or any other object you choose into a magical tool and helper. When you consecrate your talisman, you dedicate it and devote yourself to your purpose with sincerity and faith.

Rituals are sets of symbolic actions performed in a predetermined order. When you perform a ritual, you step outside the ordinary world and shift your awareness into another state. This enables you to access deeper parts of your consciousness and connects you with the collective source of wisdom and energy that we all share. You let the universe know that you're doing something significant and committed, and ask for support for a successful result.

Rituals don't have to be formal, traditional, or theatrical. They should have meaning for *you* and use language and actions that resonate with *you*. In Part II, we'll discuss the common elements of ritual and you'll have an opportunity to create a ritual that you're eager and happy to perform. When you let your creativity run free, you can craft something authentic and powerful.

Sympathetic Forces

When you create a talisman, you employ what's called "sympathetic magic," a practice grounded in the belief that like produces like, that an effect resembles its cause. That's why it's so important that, when you choose the material for your talisman, you select something that shares an affinity or characteristic or connection with your desired result so your talisman can attract it to you.

In Part II, we'll look more closely at choosing the material that is right for your talisman, but here are a couple of examples to show you what I'm getting at. If you intend to invite love into your life, choose a rose-quartz pendant, because that crystal's properties include love, self-love, and healing. Or choose a heart-shaped charm or anything that corresponds to love or symbolizes it for you. If you're seeking financial abundance, try using a money-attracting crystal like citrine or pyrite, or a shiny coin or a money clip, or a pendant shaped like a dollar sign. Anything that says wealth to you.

Ready for Some Magic?

Amulets and lucky charms will always have their place in my heart and in my pockets. But, because talismans focus on manifesting a specific intention, they are the most powerful tool for your magical work. Creating a talisman is an intimate and personal experience that inspires joy, self-discovery, and change. Rather than putting your faith in someone else's ideas or traditions, you trust yourself and your ability to manifest your desires. This process reminds you that you're a magical being with limitless potential.

As you prepare to create your own talisman, magic is already swirling around you. It flows and weaves and grows throughout this process. In the following chapters, you'll learn how to create an intention that clearly expresses your desire to the universe. You'll choose the material for your talisman that best suits you and makes your heart happy. You'll bring tarot into the mix; you'll meditate and visualize; and you'll perform a magical ritual to achieve the change you crave.

So are you ready for some magic?

MUSINGS

- How do you feel about ritual?

- How do you feel about magic?

- At this point, how do you think talismans work?

- Do you have confidence in your magical abilities?

CHAPTER 2

The Magic of Tarot

Tarot cards are magic in tangible form. When you hold a deck, you know there's more to it than paper, ink, and pretty pictures. The tarot's traditional structure and language of symbols charge the cards with meaning, purpose, and wisdom. Each tarot deck brings its own particular style, personality, and philosophy to the readings. But when you work with a deck, you add your own perspective, emotions, and experience. You form a bond and an energetic connection with the deck, just as you do with a talisman.

Tarot is an integral part of the process of creating a talisman described in this book. In the following chapters, I give you my thoughts on this ancient practice. I outline the meanings of the tarot cards, and what they can do for you. The cards are ready and willing to guide and support you, but you have to be able to communicate with them confidently. So we'll also look at different spreads and how to read them.

While you certainly don't have to be an expert to draw insights from the tarot, you do have to be able to hear what the cards have to say to you. I hope this book provides a good starting point. And no matter where you are in your tarot adventure, I'm excited to share my thoughts on the cards with you. Perhaps I can draw you into a lifelong love affair with the tarot—or, if you're already there, give you more to love.

My Love Affair with Tarot

My lifelong love affair with tarot began when, at age thirteen, I found my first tarot deck at a metaphysical store on the edge of the posh part of town. I'd come into the city with my mother, who let me wander around the shop while she enjoyed the more fashionable stores. Tarot wasn't as popular or accessible then as it is now; this was before you could order a deck online in your pajamas and have it arrive on your doorstep the next morning. So this was a thrilling day for me.

I remember dusty shelves crammed with books and decks and other strange things. Diviners sat at small tables throughout the shop, partially hidden by starry curtains and incense smoke. I was too shy even to think about having a reading done or talking to those ethereal beings. I just floated past them, hoping to catch a few words as they read for their clients.

Then I spotted a deck of cards in a black box sitting on one of the shelves. Bold white letters on the side spelled out "Tarot." And I knew I had to have that particular deck. I bought it for myself and didn't tell anyone else about it.

Those cards were my secret. I didn't keep them hidden because I thought I'd get in trouble or anything like that. I just wanted to get to know them in my own time. I didn't want to have to explain to anyone else why I liked them or what I thought I was going to do with them. That deck was just for me, and I was looking forward to many private conversations with it and many discoveries. I still have that deck, along with many more.

Some people question whether you should buy your own tarot deck. Some think you should wait until one is given to you. I don't agree—and I'm glad I didn't do that. I say go ahead and buy yourself whatever deck (or decks) attract you. You can do this at your favorite brick-and-mortar shop, or you can buy one online at midnight in your pajamas.

For years, I studied independently, devouring every book I could find on tarot and pouring myself into the images and symbols. And two things started to happen as I learned about the cards and deeply immersed myself in their world.

First, when I read the cards, I knew I was connecting with something larger than myself. Something clicked when I held the deck in my hands. I wouldn't have expressed it like this when I was thirteen, but I felt the presence of the universe, the Divine. And I knew that the messages from the cards came from this collective energy source we all share—and from myself as well, because I was a part of all that. I don't mean this to sound like a lofty, transcendent religious experience. Reading the cards was just comforting and familiar to me, and it sparked my curiosity.

Second, I realized that I could see myself in the tarot—*me* as I was in that moment and *me* as I hoped to be. Those seventy-eight cards laid out my strengths and shadows with greater compassion and clarity than I had ever experienced before. I saw where I was thriving and where I was hurting. And I got glimpses of talents, gifts, and opportunities that I had previously brushed off or ignored.

When the High Priestess appeared in my readings, I knew I could trust my intuition. When the Hermit appeared, I knew that being a quiet introvert in a noisy world was okay. When the Five of Cups showed up, I had permission to cry and grieve in my own way. The Eight of Swords showed me when I was tying myself up in knots, and that it was time for me to start thinking in a different and more empowering way. The tarot made me feel seen and inspired by possibilities.

And that's why I love it. It helps me live my life well. Its practical wisdom supports me in achieving my hopes, my dreams, and my goals—right here, right now. Reading tarot isn't about fortune-telling; it's about creating the life you desire.

How does the tarot do this? In short, the cards give us a slightly distanced, honest, and compassionate look at our true selves—powerful information, indeed. In my experience, I've found that people have trouble seeing themselves as they are. We tend to focus on our flaws, our weaknesses, or our past mistakes. We require a level of perfection from ourselves that we'd never demand from anyone else. As a result, we believe that we're unworthy or incapable of love, abundance, and happiness.

But when you read the cards, it's like looking into a mirror, complete with good lighting. Your gifts, talents, and capabilities are reflected back to you; opportunities beckon you. You see where you're flourishing and where you're making decisions from fear or anger. You discover when you're projecting your troubles onto others, or limiting yourself unnecessarily. The cards reveal when your actions or attitudes are—or aren't—in alignment with your heart, and how that's impacting your life and your goals.

The cards don't reveal your unchangeable fate. They just give you a good idea of where you're heading if you continue on your current path, making the same choices and decisions. From them, you learn to see how the past influences you. You sense the energy around you right now, and the external forces and factors that are out of your control. Patterns of which you're unaware when you're in the thick of them become clear, whether they are beneficial patterns or ones that are ready to be broken. With this knowledge in your pocket, you can decide what's next for you. Should you keep doing what you're doing? Or should you make a course adjustment with clarity and confidence?

Sounds amazing, right?

The Structure of the Tarot

Now that you've got a sense of what the cards can do, let's shift to the technical side and discuss the tarot's structure. Indeed, the tarot does have a defined structure, one that you need to honor and work within. But this structure supports rather than restricts, and gives your intuition ample room to explore, expand, and play.

A traditional tarot deck has seventy-eight cards that are divided into two main groups—the Major Arcana, which means "big secrets or mysteries," and the Minor Arcana, which means "small secrets or mysteries." Although they serve different purposes, both of these groups are crucial to the deck and the two work together. Let's examine each one more closely.

The Major Arcana

The Major Arcana is the heart of the tarot. When you're new to tarot, these are the cards that are most likely to capture your heart and your imagination. Most people immediately recognize many of the archetypes represented on these cards. Some they love; some they find daunting; some take time to get to know.

There are twenty-two cards in the Major Arcana, numbered from zero to twenty-one. They represent the milestones, lessons, and life-changing experiences we encounter throughout our lives. They bring opportunities for growth and transformation, but that's not to say they're all sunshine and rainbows (although some are). Pay close attention when these cards appear in your tarot readings, because they always deliver a significant and helpful message.

The story told by the cards in the Major Arcana is often called the "Fool's journey." Life, they tell us, is a journey and, when we start on our path, we're all the Fool. The Fool card is numbered zero because the Fool is everything and nothing—pure potential with no experience or knowledge. As we go through life, we meet and embody the other twenty-one Major Arcana archetypes. We learn from them; we grow as we experience highs and lows, challenges and triumphs; we move through them toward our highest personal development.

In an ideal world, you would proceed on your Fool's journey in a neat, linear fashion, from one archetype to the next, learning all you need to know. But life isn't usually that tidy. Sometimes you go two steps forward and one step back. Sometimes you have to repeat an experience in order to learn from it. Sometimes you spend too long in one archetype or avoid another as long as you can. Nevertheless, you can trust that you'll make it to the final card—called the World—and rejoice in who you've become and what you've achieved. Then you level up and start again as a wiser Fool.

In the next chapter, you'll meet the Major Arcana archetypes one by one. For now, I encourage you to release any stereotypes or clichés you may have encountered about the tarot. Death doesn't bring doom and gloom, and the Lovers don't guarantee that your soulmate is about to appear. Let your intuition guide you to the deeper and more personal meaning of the cards. Approach the Major Arcana archetypes with the openness and curiosity of the Fool.

Living in a world governed solely by the Major Arcana, however, would be exhausting. So it's lucky that we have the Minor Arcana to give us balance. While the Major Arcana cards represent significant life events and milestones, the Minor Arcana cards help us navigate day-to-day life one step at a time.

The Minor Arcana

The cards in the Minor Arcana represent all aspects of daily life. They indicate situations that are within your control to direct or navigate, rather than the significant events represented by the Major Arcana. And while they aren't as flashy, they are a crucial part of the deck and have their own beauty.

These cards illustrate who you are as a human being getting on with life. They show your worries, your challenges, and your victories. They are the people that you love and those with whom you clash. They reveal how you manage the practical pressures and joys of daily life. The Major Arcana archetypes inspire and teach you; the Minor Arcana shows you how you can put that wisdom into practice.

In a traditional deck, the Minor Arcana is composed of four suits: Wands, Cups, Swords, and Pentacles. Each suit contains cards numbered from Ace to Ten, plus four Court Cards called Pages, Knights, Queens, and Kings. Each of the four suits represents a specific aspect of the human experience and is linked to an element to help you understand their nature and work with their themes. Wands are associated with Fire; Cups are associated with Water; Swords are associated with Air; Pentacles are associated with Earth. Let's look at the general meanings of these suits before we drill down into the specific meaning of each card.

Wands

Wands are connected to the element of Fire. They represent passion, creativity, ambition, and the desire to expand. This suit is the spark that lights you up and inspires you to burn bright and fully engage with life. Wands are your spirit.

Like fire, Wands move fast. Fire is unpredictable and, while it can sustain life, it can also be devastatingly destructive when it runs wild. Fire flames in your veins; it burns you out; it encourages hot-headed behavior.

Wands are depicted as tree branches or sticks. Even though they've been cut off, however, they sprout fresh green leaves that are full of life. A wand can be a staff on which to lean or a weapon when you need to protect your boundaries. It can be a magic wand in your hand, waiting for you to use. Wands hold ground and mark territory, but are always flexible enough to bend rather than break.

When you align with the suit of Wands, you have the confidence to pursue your passions and act on divinely inspired ideas, as well as the courage and resilience to accomplish those ambitions. Wands often appear in areas of life like careers, entrepreneurial ventures, creative projects, and anything (or anyone) that sets your soul on fire.

Cups

Cups are connected to the element of Water. They represent your emotions, intuition, and compassion, and anything you love. This suit inspires you to fall in love, to get your heart broken, and to follow impossible dreams. Cups are your heart.

Like water, Cups replenish and keep us flowing. But don't forget that water can be a gentle stream, a soft rain, a raging hurricane, or an ocean of unknowable depths—just as your emotions sometimes overflow with joy or overwhelm you like a tidal wave. Cups are happy tears, sorrowful weeping, and the beating of your heart. Rather than drowning in the Cups, it's best to float with the ebb and flow.

Cups are vessels. They hold, contain, and receive; you can offer your cup to someone else or share a drink. When your cup is full or overflowing, you're happy. When it's empty, you feel drained or hollow. Whether your cup is half-empty or half-full always depends on your heart and how you experience love.

When you align with the suit of Cups, you understand your heart's desires. Relationships with loved ones improve, and you can break old patterns that bring repeated heartbreak. Cups teach you how to love yourself better and empathize with others. They often come up in readings centered on relationships, love, self-love, and pursuing your soul's purpose.

Swords

Swords are connected to the element of Air. They are your thoughts, your words, your unwavering determination to find answers and understand how things work. This suit is the cold wind that blows away mental cobwebs, challenges your beliefs, and urges you to say what needs to be said. Swords are your mind.

Like air, this suit can be clear or cloudy. We can't survive very long without air, and a deep breath can clear your mind and center you. But air can also be a tornado that sends you airborne or a gust that blows dust in your eyes. Air focuses your vision, makes you light-headed, and encourages lofty ideas. Whenever you pinpoint what's going on in a situation or see right through people's masks and facades, that's the suit of Swords at work.

Swords are depicted as shining, cold, and intimidating. A sword can be a helpful tool, a defender, or a deadly weapon. Like our words, swords may be double-edged, razor-sharp, or blunt. Like our thoughts, they can wound or be a powerful resource. Swords want you to get to the point and clear the air;

they cut ties and offer truth that may hurt as well as victory. It takes strength, courage, and conviction to pick up a sword and take on the challenge it offers.

When you align with the suit of Swords, clarity of mind is your superpower. You can make decisions firmly based on logic, facts, and your moral compass. Communication becomes clearer, leading to conflict resolution and speaking authentically. Swords often come up for areas of life like communication, conflict, ethics, writing and study, and anything that stimulates the intellect.

Pentacles

Pentacles are connected to the element of Earth. They relate to material aspects of life that contribute to your security and comfort, like your job, your home, your finances, and your physical well-being. They are also all the plants and creatures that live and grow in nature and enjoy the earth's abundance. This suit gives you the strength to carry your responsibilities on your shoulders and encourages you to put down roots and enjoy the results of hard work. Pentacles are your body.

Like the earth, Pentacles move slowly. Like seeds planted in the ground, Pentacles can't be rushed or bullied into blooming at an accelerated speed. Earth is fertile and you can usually count on it being solid beneath your feet. But it can also be mud you get stuck in or a quake that rattles your foundations. Earth grounds you, reminds you that you're mortal, and encourages you to enjoy the pleasures of the physical world while you're here.

Pentacles are depicted as gold coins inscribed with a five-pointed star. Coins are a resource that you can spend now or invest in yourself and your future. If you manage them well, they can multiply and support you in creating an abundant lifestyle. But if you hold coins too tightly or hide them under your mattress, you will feel scarcity and lack. Moreover, if you focus on Pentacles solely as money, you lose the magic of growth and may feel cut off from your spiritual side.

When you align with the suit of Pentacles, you can manifest your desires through consistent action and slow growth; you can pace yourself and enjoy life's simple pleasures. Pentacles appear in areas of life like work, health and well-being, projects that take time, and a connection with the natural world.

Numbers

While the elements connected with the suits of the Minor Arcana provide valuable information, so do the numbers on each card. These numbers have their own innate meanings, but they can also reveal the progression of a story.

- Aces represent a gift, a beginning, or potential.

- Twos indicate choices, balance, or partnership.

- Threes show integration, creativity, or expansion.

- Fours speak to stability, structure, or foundation.

- Fives reveal conflict, struggle, or challenge.

- Sixes point to harmony, generosity, or balance.

- Sevens signal adjustment, resourcefulness, or reflection.

- Eights reflect movement, commitment, or skill.

- Nines imply culmination, intensity, or contemplation.

- Tens denote completion, success, or evolution.

Just as the Major Arcana cards tell the story of the Fool's journey, the Minor Arcana can reveal whether you're at the beginning of a situation, in the messy middle, or close to the end.

For example, a cluster of Aces can indicate that you're about to start something new. Tens appear when you're close to achieving your goal or ending a situation. Fives indicate a time of challenge and the decision to persevere or to quit. Pay attention to numbers when reading the cards—especially if they repeat.

The Court Cards

The Court Cards are traditionally called Pages, Knights, Queens, and Kings. They are ranked in a hierarchy rather than by numbers, and the scenes on the cards are simple—figures holding the emblem of their suit. Although these images are simple, however, the Court Cards are anything but. Why? Because they represent people, with all their unique personality traits, motivations, and backstories.

Most of the time, the Court Cards represent you. They illustrate your role in a particular situation; they show you how you're behaving and whether that's beneficial. Depending on where they appear in a reading, they may offer valuable guidance on an attitude or approach that can help you achieve your goal or respond to a challenge. They give you perspective on yourself. They reveal the strengths and abilities you have, as well as patterns that may or may not serve you well.

While it is generally safe to assume that a Court Card represents you, that may not always be the case. If you are confident that the card does *not* reflect you—based on its characteristics or position in a spread—it may be that someone else is showing up in the reading. This makes sense if you're asking about relationships, family, work, or community dynamics.

Because the traditional depictions of the Court Cards clearly express gender, age, and rank, they may appear in more inclusive forms in many modern decks. No matter which deck you use, I encourage you to look beneath the surface details of these cards and get to their essential energy. Anyone can be a King or a Queen; anyone can be called upon at any time to play the part of a Knight or a Page. And all these roles are valuable and powerful in their own unique ways. As you read the brief descriptions below of the energy of these cards, keep in mind the characteristics of their suit, their element, and their rank.

- *Pages* have youthful energy. They approach the world like children, curious and full of delight. Having no experience or expectations, they are open and want to learn. They'll make mistakes, but that's all part of their growth and development. Regardless of age, if you show up as a Page, you're acting or feeling like a kid. Perhaps you're a student or starting something new; perhaps you often look to others for guidance and reassurance.

- *Knights* have boundless energy. They crave action and movement, and aren't concerned with the distant future. Their idealistic outlook spurs them on to impossible quests, but they're restless and changeable.

Knights are most successful when focused on short-term goals; multi-tasking isn't for them. These go-getters want to prove themselves and win the prize.

- *Queens* have mature, compassionate energy. They know the importance of nurturing themselves and they generously support the flourishing of others. Although they've reached a high level of leadership and responsibility, they seek expansion and growth, and their creativity flows easily. Queens know themselves well and are entirely at home in their element.

- *Kings* have mature, stable energy. They focus on consolidating their achievements and maintaining their position. They're wary of the risks and possible instability that come with change. Their priority will always be the greater good, because they take their role and responsibilities seriously. Kings expect to be heard and obeyed.

ABOUT REVERSALS

When a tarot card appears upside down in a reading, it is called a "reversal." There are many different ways to interpret a reversed card. Some choose simply to disregard them completely. Others think they turn the meaning of the card on its head, signifying a blockage or challenge related to the card's theme. The interpretation of reversed cards is entirely dependent on the context of a reading and your own creative ideas. If you choose to consider reversals in your readings, sit with the card and find the interpretation that feels right to you.

Personally, I don't read with reversals. Upright cards have so many levels of meaning and are so rich in nuance that they tell the whole story. But if a card manages to reverse itself even though I keep my deck upright and shuffle in a way that maintains that position, I pay attention. In this case, my approach is not to see the card's meaning as completely opposite, but rather to assume that the card wants to stand out and be seen because its energy is blocked or out of balance, or the timing isn't right.

If reversals resonate with you, by all means use them in your regular practice and when you create talismans. If you do decide to use them, however, just be clear on what they signify to you in a reading, and stick with that system.

Clearing and Bonding with Your Cards

Tarot cards are magical tools. When you practice magic, the power comes from you, but your tools support you and amplify your skills and intention. When this happens, it becomes a joy to work together. If you give your cards care, energy, and respect, they'll give that right back to you.

I suggest keeping your deck on a tidy shelf in a nice bag to keep it safe and clean. This doesn't have to be made of an expensive fabric or be of a particular color. Just pick a material or a pattern that speaks to you. And when you get a new deck, be sure to clear it of any residual energy before working with it. You can also do this to reconnect with a deck you haven't worked with for a while, or with a deck you use regularly for yourself and others. This keeps the energy flowing so that your readings don't bleed into each other, and ensures that the echoes of emotion and insights don't influence new readings.

Here's a short list of ways to clear your cards.

- Keep a clear quartz crystal or a piece of selenite in the bag with your cards, or place one on top of the deck when you're not using it.

- Ring a bell or chime a singing bowl over and around your cards.

- Thoroughly shuffle your deck or put the cards back in order.

- Hold the deck and imagine you're infusing it with white light.

- Leave your cards in the light of a Full Moon overnight.

- Waft each card, or the whole deck, through incense smoke.

Try some of these methods and see what resonates most with you.

Once you have cleared your deck, you can begin to bond with it. This doesn't require elaborate practices; just enjoy spending time with your deck. Handle it often and use it frequently. Get to know how it feels in your hands and what the images evoke for you. This brings your energies in line with those of the cards.

One quick and practical way to do this is to pull a card each morning and ask: "How can I make the most of this day?" Or: "What do I need to know today?" Spend some time with the card and make notes about how it makes you feel. What aspect of the card jumps out at you? How does it relate to your current situation? At the end of the day, revisit your card and reflect on how it appeared to you or make notes in your journal.

Or perhaps you prefer working with meditation. In that case, focus your meditation on a card—perhaps the card you pulled that morning or a card you want to get to know better. You can also put a card under your pillow (carefully, so it doesn't get damaged) and ask for a dream to help you understand the card's message. And, of course, read the guidebook that came with your deck, and every other tarot book that catches your interest. Take notes as you read, including what you want to remember and any discoveries you want to explore further.

Again, there are many ways of bonding with your deck. Find one that has meaning for you. Remember, tarot has no hard and fast rules. That's one of the reasons why I love it.

MUSINGS

- Why do you read tarot? Or, if you're just starting out, why do you want to read tarot?

- Try several of the methods for clearing and bonding with your cards.

- Separate the Major Arcana cards from your tarot deck and arrange them in order from zero to twenty-one. Using your intuition and imagination, tell yourself the story of the Fool's journey. If you're stuck, start with: "Once upon a time, a Fool..." Then go from there, through all the cards. Notice which ones resonate with you. Which ones spark your curiosity? Which ones repel you?

- Which of the Minor Arcana's four elements feels most comfortable or pleasurable for you? Does one feel uncomfortable? Confusing? Neutral? Ask yourself why.

CHAPTER 3

The Major Arcana

The twenty-two cards of the Major Arcana represent the milestones, lessons, and transformational experiences we encounter throughout our lives. These archetypes will capture your imagination immediately, but it takes time to get to know them deeply. There are always more layers to discover. As you work with them, you'll create connections, build narratives, and develop meanings. In this chapter, I offer my interpretations of these cards based on my own experiences. Take them as a starting point, and as an invitation to create your own relationship with these nuanced archetypes.

The cards of the Major Arcana tell you stories—like a favorite teacher or a loved one who always has time to sit down with you and share their memories and wisdom. Studying and learning about them are essential to reading the tarot, but don't make this arduous work. You don't have to learn all twenty-two cards at once, and you don't need to learn them in order to commit them all to memory.

The descriptions I give you here will help you read the spreads that follow with confidence, accuracy, and insight, and guide you as you perform the practices in the rest of the book. You'll work closely with these meanings as you create your talisman. For each card, I give you a description that explores the scenes and symbols that appear on it, and an interpretation of what the card signifies in a reading. Then I offer possible themes for your talisman's intention as suggested by the cards. Refer to these when doing the one-card reading described in chapter 6 and the tarot spread given in chapter 10. I also suggest affirmations for each card—powerful and positive statements that encapsulate and activate the card's energy in you. You can refer to these for inspiration and examples as you create your own affirmations later in the book. Finally, I give musings to spark reflection, encourage new perspectives, and stimulate curiosity about the meaning of each card.

0—The Fool

The Fool is poised at the edge of a cliff. He's about to step off, unfazed by the precipitous drop ahead. It doesn't occur to him to look before he leaps; he keeps his eyes on the sky. The Fool is on the brink of an adventure and unprepared for it, but he's got a feeling that, no matter what happens, it will be wonderful.

The Fool travels with a small bag over his shoulder, dressed in pretty clothing that is unmarred by the dust, dirt, and sweat of the road. He delicately holds a white rose that reveals his innocence; the red feather in his cap shows his passion and vitality. The mountains in the distance hint at future challenges, dangers, and opportunities for achievement, but the Fool isn't concerned with the future.

He lives in the present moment. He's got a faithful companion—a little white dog who's up for whatever sticky situations and marvelous adventures his master encounters.

- *Card interpretation:* The Fool represents new beginnings and pure potential. He's numbered zero, offering you a fresh start, free of baggage or expectations. All you have to do is take a leap of faith to get things rolling. Throw yourself into unknown territory, trusting in the benevolence of the universe and your own resourcefulness, rather than trying to plan out all the details. If you knew how challenging it would be, you might not do it and that would be a shame, because you'd miss out on something magnificent. Risk is involved, but synchronicities and serendipities will guide you. Luck will follow you, and unexpected gifts will land in your lap. So dive in.

- *Talisman intention themes:* Taking a leap of faith, starting something new, trusting in the universe, reinventing yourself.

- *Affirmation:* My life is an adventure.

- *Musings:* When did you last take a leap of faith? How did things turn out?

1—THE MAGICIAN

When the Magician performs his mesmerizing tricks, you can't look away. Magic wand firmly in hand, he dazzles his audience with his sharp gaze and his precise movements. The most thrilling part of the show is that, deep down, you know these aren't tricks at all; the Magician really can work magic.

THE MAGICIAN.

The Magician is a master of manifestation. When he raises his wand to the heavens, power flows through him. When he points to the earth and uses his force of will, he shapes that energy into whatever he desires. He has his tools laid out on his table, ready to use. You may recognize symbols of the four suits of the Minor Arcana—a wand, a cup, a sword, and a coin—representing the four elements of Fire, Water, Air, and Earth. The Magician has intention, focus, and the skills he needs for success. The infinity symbol above his head and the ouroboros around his waist signify access to limitless power and possibilities. If he can imagine it, he can make it so.

- *Card interpretation:* The Magician shines a green light from the universe, signaling you to use your magic and power. If you've been holding back from something you have been meaning to do or start or try, now is the time to act. You don't need to take another class, or get another qualification, or wait until the stars align. You have all the talents, skills, and experience you need to achieve your goal. Just do it! Get out of your own way and show your awesome powers to the world. When you focus your attention and act, you can accomplish anything.

- *Talisman intention themes:* Using your skills, showing your talents, marketing, manifestation, performance, magical work.

- *Affirmation:* I am a master of manifestation.

- *Musings:* Remember a time when you pulled a rabbit out of a hat and surprised yourself with your talent or skill. How did that feel?

2—The High Priestess

HIGH PRIESTESS.

Most tarot readers are in love with the High Priestess. She is the all-knowing and all-seeing mystic we secretly want to be. She communicates through visions and dreams, and travels easily beyond the veil to the world of spirit. Like a great tarot reader, she'll accompany you on a journey into the deepest shadows of your soul, while allowing you to discover your truths on your own.

The High Priestess wears a triple-moon crown. The waxing, full, and waning moons move through their phases above her head. A crescent moon rests at her feet, and her robe pours around her like water. These symbols place her firmly in the realm of intuition and Divine Feminine wisdom, and she trusts those forces above all else.

The Priestess sits balanced between black and white columns, honoring both the shadow and the light in us all. The veil behind her is covered in pomegranates and palm leaves, representing fertility, and we get a glimpse of water beyond it. The scroll she holds in her lap is tightly rolled and tucked partially into her robe. She only reveals her mysteries when you're ready to see and understand them.

- *Card interpretation:* Believe in yourself and implicitly trust your inner voice. Your intuition will provide the information you need right now, and your compassionate and wise heart will inform you of the best course of action. Be observant; listen more than speak; notice the details others miss. You're a natural diviner on a spiritual path, with the goal and reward of knowing yourself well. Your ability to see right through to people's hearts and motivations can be lonely. But ultimately, it's better to know the truth and be honest with yourself about how you want to proceed. Keep your cards close to your chest. You don't need to reveal the mysteries and insights you discover. Not everyone is ready to hear what you have to say.

- *Talisman intention themes:* Divination, trusting your intuition, connecting with the Divine Feminine, following a spiritual path.

- *Affirmation:* I trust my inner voice.

- *Musings:* How do you distinguish your intuition from your logical mind? How does your intuition manifest? As a feeling in your body? As a voice or vision? Or as something else?

3—THE EMPRESS

The Empress is the Earth Mother and the goddess of love and beauty. She is abundance, compassion, sensuality, and the force that inspires every creature on earth to thrive and grow. Everything she touches flourishes.

The Empress rests comfortably in her power, wearing a starry crown and brandishing a scepter as emblems of her sovereignty in heaven and on earth. Her

THE EMPRESS.

throne is piled with luxurious cushions, and she resides deep in the heart of lush nature, not in a cold palace. Water flows toward her, grain ripe for harvest leans in her direction, and the lush green trees behind her support and protect her. The pomegranates adorning her gown represent fertility; the symbol of Venus appears on her shield. There's a hint that she may be pregnant, or certainly in the full bloom of health and vitality. The scene on the card is bursting with luscious life, suggesting that something is about to be born—perhaps a new life, a creative project, or a passionate relationship.

- *Card interpretation:* When the Empress appears, she invites you to feel your power and glory in your Divine Feminine energy. Enjoy sensual pleasures in the here and now. Appreciate your physical body and do what feels good for the sake of it. Eat and drink well; admire or create works of art and music; get outside and breathe in the scent of blossoms, green leaves, and ripe fruit. Like the Empress, you are a leader who rules with love. Your compassion, generosity, and concern for the well-being of others in your care are boundless and fierce. You are always ready to comfort, to give good advice, and to protect your dear ones. But be sure to lavish that same love and care on yourself so you can continue to thrive and grow, and cultivate an even greater capacity for joy.

- *Talisman intention themes:* Sovereignty, self-love, birthing a creative project, loving and nurturing your body.

- *Affirmation:* I am the creator of my rich and abundant life.

- *Musings:* Do you feel comfortable and connected with your physical body? How do you nurture yourself?

4—The Emperor

Time and the weight of a heavy crown have taken their toll on the Emperor. His white hair and impressive beard show how long he has occupied his throne, overseeing his empire and keeping it safe and secure. He holds an ankh-shaped scepter in one hand and an orb in the other, symbols of his life-long commitment and vast power as ruler.

THE EMPEROR.

Although we can't see any impending threats in this scene, the Emperor wears armor under his heavy red cloak. His eyes are on the horizon and he remains in a constant state of vigilance. He sits on a solid, angular stone throne that's not meant for lounging or comfort—very different from the Empress's cozy cushions! Even the rams' heads that decorate the throne look off in different directions, as if they're also watching for danger.

The Emperor values security and control. He'd rather maintain his stark, rocky empire than nurture or expand it. He takes his responsibilities to his subjects seriously, but he values the greater good over individual happiness. Those who break his rules suffer the consequences.

- *Card interpretation:* It's not easy being a good Emperor. You have responsibilities; people rely on you; you have to make decisions using your hard head rather than your soft heart. As you do this, be aware of how you use your power—the world needs benevolent rulers more than it needs tyrants. Think back on times when you had to defer to an authority figure and remember what it felt like to be guided by a strong leader rather than subject to an inept one. Structure, order, and a solid foundation are your best friends right now, so if you don't have those in place, start building them.

- *Talisman intention themes:* Security, structure, upholding your responsibilities, building your career or business, being a good leader.

- *Affirmation:* I take care of my empire.

- *Musings:* Are you comfortable with leadership? How do you feel when you're subject to someone else's rules?

5—THE HIEROPHANT

The Hierophant has an intense gaze, but it doesn't feel as if he sees us. He looks above and beyond, privy to miracles and mysteries we can't see. He is like a pope, or a priest, or a preacher—an intermediary between us and the Divine.

THE HIEROPHANT.

His ceremonial regalia, his crown, and his staff confirm the Hierophant's place in heaven and his authority on earth. He raises his hand in benediction, blessing the two acolytes at his feet who are eager to soak in his words of wisdom and provide whatever service he may need.

The Hierophant is a sage teacher and spiritual guide. He holds the keys to knowledge and will open the world to you. But sometimes he is the kind of teacher who isn't so fond of being asked questions or offered alternative viewpoints. He'll tell you how the world works; he'll teach you your place in it and what is expected of you. And he wants you to listen and remember.

- *Card interpretation:* The Hierophant represents tradition, conventional wisdom, and familial or societal expectations. Consider the roles these institutions play in your life when he appears in your cards. Are they supportive and relevant? Or are they limiting beliefs you need to shift? This card invites you to honor and learn from the teachers you encounter throughout the years and to assimilate the knowledge they offer. Then it encourages you to ask yourself what their lessons mean to you in the progression of your life path and purpose. You have valuable wisdom to share, and there are people around you who want to hear what you have to say. Be ready to step into a role as teacher as well.

- *Talisman intention themes:* Teaching, mentoring, education, traditions, accessing spiritual guidance.

- *Affirmation:* I am a seeker of truth.

- *Musings:* Can you recall teachers who impacted your life? What did you learn from them?

6—THE LOVERS

Most people are happy when the Lovers card appears. It denotes the feeling of astonishment, gratitude, and butterflies in the stomach that we experience when we sense a deep love for another person or for the Divine, and even for ourselves.

A bright sun fills the scene on this card, as a fiery angel blesses two naked humans who hold out their hands in awe and reverence. We see Adam and Eve in the Garden of Eden, but the angel with the sword isn't driving them out. They are protected and cherished. The snake coiled around the Tree of the Knowledge of Good and Evil murmurs in Eve's ear, but her eyes are fixed on the Divine above. Adam gazes at her, seemingly unaware of the presence of the angel hovering right above him.

The Lovers card illustrates human nature. We all have masculine, femi-nine, and divine energy within us; we are all beings of body, mind, and spirit. We transform and ascend when we love and unite all parts of ourselves.

- *Card interpretation:* If you are in a relationship, this card bodes well. It represents an authentic connection between two people and the potential for this partnership to go even deeper. If you're looking for love, this card lets you know that the real thing is out there and is worth seeking. However, remember that its message is likely not about romance at all. It can invite you to seek harmony within your heart and mind, and reach a place where you love all aspects of yourself. When you love yourself well, the universe sends love right back to you. The Lovers also carries an older and hidden meaning related to choice. It reminds you that your choices have consequences for yourself and for those you love. When this card appears, make the decision that aligns with your heart and values, and follow the path of love.

- *Talisman intention themes:* Seeking love or a soulmate, fostering self-love, connecting with angels and the Divine, making heart-centered choices, unity.

- *Affirmation:* Love informs my decisions.

- *Musings:* How well do you love yourself? How does your self-love impact your relationships?

7—THE CHARIOT

Once it gets going, the Chariot is an unstoppable juggernaut. The charioteer is in the driver's seat, ready to leave behind what's safe and familiar in his life and make his fortune. He still has much to learn, but, based on past successes, he has the confidence to navigate the road ahead—including any potholes and unexpected detours.

The Chariot is a bright and cheerful card, but mysterious details reveal themselves when you look closely. Notice the stars on the canopy above the charioteer and on his crown, and the moons on his shoulders. There are planetary symbols on his belt and glyphs on his kilt. His staff looks like a magic wand. His chariot is pulled by mythical sphinxes rather than horses, and getting them to agree to pull in the direction he desires is no small feat. He is a victorious warrior, but he also has access to divine guidance, intuition, and a greater purpose than he may realize at the outset of his journey.

THE CHARIOT.

- *Card interpretation:* Have confidence in yourself. When the Chariot appears, it's time to move full steam ahead in your life. You're ready for a challenge, and you have momentum. Why not make the most of it and go faster and farther? Keep in mind, however, that although you don't have to map out your entire journey, you do need to have a target or goal. If you do, you'll undoubtedly reach it. If you don't, you may go around in circles for a while, go off-roading, or take a much more scenic route than you intended. You're about to move forward, but how can you ever reach your destination if you don't know where you're going?

- *Talisman intention themes:* Independence, confidence, opening the road forward, travel, relocating, navigating challenges, achieving success.

- *Affirmation:* I direct the course of my life with confidence and skill.

- *Musings:* Are you being pulled in different directions? How can you resolve that conflict and focus on one goal?

8—Strength

In the scene on this card, a woman in white with flowers in her hair subdues a lion. When she closes the lion's jaws with gentle and steady hands, he turns into a trusting puppy, with his tail between his legs. Like a mother calming an agitated child, she soothes; but she doesn't put up with any nonsense, snarling, or biting. Strength is a lion tamer with a heart. Instead of a whip and a chair, she relies on compassion and patience to calm that noble cat.

Despite the danger inherent in encountering a lion, this woman radiates grace and composure, knowing she has the situation well in hand. She has endless reserves of inner fortitude that are constantly renewed and flow like the infinity symbol above her head. The mountain behind her represents the path of strength—taking the high road rather than relying on aggression or ego, in full awareness of how far it will test her limits.

- *Card interpretation:* When Strength appears, challenges lie ahead, or you may already be in the thick of them. Face them with trust in your capacity to manage any difficulties that come your way. You know you are strong and, in fact, you have even deeper resources of inner strength available to you, ready to be accessed when you need them. To gain insight into the nature of the coming challenges, ask yourself who or what the lion represents in your life. If a partner, family member, friend, or colleague is lashing out at you, offer them understanding and care, but don't let them disrupt your serenity or draw you into conflict. If you are dealing with an external situation, manage it with firm pressure and confidence. And if you discover that the lion is you, be kind to yourself. Acknowledge what is causing your pain, anger, or frustration, without allowing your ego to terrorize the countryside. A lion is majestic, courageous, and bold—an expression of your lust for life. Don't try to domesticate that force; learn how to channel it in productive and enriching ways.

- **Talisman intention themes:** Managing challenges, accessing inner strength, keeping your poise under pressure.

- **Affirmation:** I am lion-hearted.

- **Musings:** Do you perform well under pressure? What strengths do you call upon in times of stress or conflict?

9—THE HERMIT

The Hermit lives alone on an icy mountain peak, far from noise, people, and distractions. The harshness of the location discourages visitors, and he doesn't miss the comforts and diversions of city life. The Hermit needs solitude to contemplate the meaning of life in peace. His lonely path isn't for the faint of heart. The wisdom he seeks lies deep within, and it takes courage and discipline to journey there.

THE HERMIT.

The Hermit is the curmudgeonly sage, the wizard, or the scholar that you know from many folk tales—the one who'd rather stay in his cave or forest hovel with his books. But he is also a wise teacher and mentor, and he knows that others desperately need the knowledge he discovers. He holds a shining lantern high to guide students and seekers, venturing back into the world from time to time.

- *Card interpretation:* Life is often busy and noisy, and it's easy to become disconnected or just go through the motions each day. When you crave time alone to reflect, to reconnect, and to make sense of your thoughts and feelings, take it. You may not be seeking answers to the mysteries of the universe; you may just yearn to recharge with a good book or pay a solitary visit to a favorite place. If you're working on a project that needs all your attention right now, let loved ones or colleagues know that you will be unavailable for the foreseeable future, and that it's nothing personal. Retreat to your hermit's cave to find perspective and helpful guidance. You'll have wisdom to share when you emerge.

- *Talisman intention themes:* Writing, studying, finding or being a mentor, understanding life purpose, self-knowledge.

- *Affirmation:* I have a universe of knowledge to discover within myself.

- *Musings:* Do you enjoy your own company? What activities do you prefer to do alone? Why?

10—The Wheel of Fortune

At first glance, the Wheel of Fortune seems overwhelming. A sword-bearing sphinx sits on top of the wheel and the Egyptian god Anubis cradles it from below, while a snake undulates down the side. Four winged figures read books and lounge on clouds in the corners of the card, and the wheel itself, which occupies center stage, is covered in enigmatic symbols. Before you attempt to break down all these symbols, take a moment to appreciate the magnificent atmosphere of mystery this card conveys.

There are two sets of letters in the outer ring that spell out "tarot," or "taro." But they also spell "tora," the Hebrew book of God's wisdom and law, and "rota," which is Latin for "wheel." The Tetragrammaton, the unutterable name of God, appears between those letters. Alchemical symbols are inscribed in the center of the wheel—mercury, sulfur, water, and salt. The four creatures in the corners are often associated with the four fixed signs of the Zodiac—Aquarius (the angel), Scorpio (the eagle), Leo (the lion), and Taurus (the bull). Anubis is a helper who conducts souls to the afterlife. Depending on your perspective, the snake represents rebirth, transformation, or danger. The sphinx invites you to answer her riddle so that you can move forward, but she won't give you any hints.

This mysterious card can be destabilizing. It brings luck and opportunities, as well as uncertainty and the unknown. But one thing you know for sure is that this card brings change. What will that look like? Well, you'll have to wait and see. The Wheel of Fortune gives you a glimpse into the pattern of your life, but it doesn't reveal all. Yet.

WHEEL OF FORTUNE. 4

- *Card interpretation:* When I read tarot, I always stress that we have free will. We make our own decisions, and our futures aren't entirely set in stone. The Wheel of Fortune is the one card that throws that idea for a loop. When this card appears, all you can do is hang on and see where it takes you. If you've been feeling blocked in some area, it lets you know the situation is ready to shift and move. Watch for opportunities and decide quickly whether you're going to seize them or not. These are limited-time offers. If you don't jump on them, the wheel will turn, and you'll have to wait for them to come around again. The Wheel of Fortune is also a force of karma. What goes around comes around, for good or evil. If you're down, know you may be going up, and vice versa. Make the best of what life throws at you. No state of being is permanent.

- *Talisman intention themes:* Good luck, good timing, risks paying off, fate and destiny, solving a puzzling problem.

- *Affirmation:* Luck is on my side.

- *Musings:* When did you last take a risk or a gamble? Did it pay off?

11—JUSTICE

In the tarot, Justice isn't blind. She uses her clear vision and golden scales to weigh your actions, carefully considering all sides of the story. Her upright sword never wavers, for she has confidence in herself and her judgment, and won't be swayed from the truth. Once she comes to her verdict, you're subject to the consequences. Her decision will be fair, and you'll get what you deserve—whether that's a reassuring or a distressing proposition.

Justice wears a red robe and a heavy crown, showing her authority and how seriously she takes her responsibilities. Her pose is as balanced as her decisions. She sits between two sturdy columns, showing the power and stability of universal law. But these columns aren't black and white like those on the High Priestess card. They are gray.

- *Card interpretation:* When Justice appears, she requires that you be honest with yourself, judge your past actions and current circumstances with a neutral eye, and take responsibility for them. This may feel uncomfortable, but it's necessary to ensure that you're in balance with who you are and what you stand for. If you don't know these things, it's a good time to figure them out. The next time you make an important decision, rely on logic and facts rather than emotion. Weigh the pros and cons before you commit, and be sure you're clear about your motivations. The most beneficial choices will be those that are compatible with your ethics and your life purpose. But they won't necessarily be the easiest.

- *Talisman intention themes:* Karma, resolving past mistakes, favorable legal outcomes, resolution of unfair situations, activism, advocacy.

- *Affirmation:* My principles guide my actions.

- *Musings:* Are you waiting for justice in some area of your life? Where? Why?

12—THE HANGED ONE

Your first impulse may be to turn this card around so the figure is right-side up. But when you take a closer look, you realize that this won't work. By turn-ing the card, you put the hanging figure in an even more improbable position. The Hanged One is exactly where he needs to be.

THE HANGED ONE. ♆

The figure on this card is in a strange pose, yet he shows no signs of distress. He looks relaxed, even serene. He hangs upside down from a tree by his ankle, but his other leg is crossed at a jaunty angle and his arms rest behind his back. We don't know if his hands are tied, but the ease of his posture gives the impres-sion that they aren't. He's waiting for something, but he knows it is coming. So there's no need to be impatient and no way to hurry things up.

His eyes are open wide, gathering informa-tion, and he exudes a dreamy feeling of tran-scendence. His glowing halo reveals that he's becoming enlightened through this process and has reached a state of grace and detachment.

- *Card interpretation:* The Hanged One asks you to surrender, release, and let go. Just *be.* There is nothing effective that you can do right now, so relax, hang back, and observe how events unfold. This may feel uncomfortable or seem like a sacrifice, but there's no point in pushing forward and wasting your energy. You'll benefit the most from this time by looking at life from a different perspective so the solutions and insights you need can present themselves to you. Be at ease in your life, in this moment, because this is where you need to be.

- *Talisman intention themes:* Meditation, new perspective, surrender, enlightenment.

- *Affirmation:* I know when to let go.

- *Musings:* Is stillness uncomfortable for you? Do you find it difficult to release control of any situations in your life?

13—Death

Death is formidable. His skull face grins. His eye sockets are empty. His bony fingers threaten. The red eyes of his elegant horse are also frightening and unnatural. There is no doubt that these are two creatures of death and the underworld, not living beings to whom we can relate. They remind us of our own mortality. They force us to confront the fact that our lives on earth are short and fleeting.

But Death rides a white horse and carries a flag bearing a white rose. He offers a greeting, a truce, and an invitation to join his parade. He is not evil or malicious, and his intentions are pure. He reminds us to make the most of our time in this human form, because he eventually comes to everyone. Death in the tarot is not the end. The sun rises in the distance.

- *Card interpretation:* Death brings profound change and transformation, ushering in a new phase of life. The price of rebirth, however, is that something must die—figuratively speaking. Death may manifest as the end of a romantic relationship or friendship. You may quit your job or mourn the end of a career path. Possessions that weigh you down may have to go, as well as old stories that hold you back. You may say goodbye to the person you thought you were, or give up a role you've played for most of your life. But these deaths are liberating. They take you down to your bare bones and allow you to focus on what matters. The bottom line is that death represents change, and change is inevitable. Will you surrender and embrace it? Or will you resist and draw out the process?

- *Talisman intention themes:* Transformation, rebirth, endings, healing grief.

- *Affirmation:* I use my time well.

- *Musings:* What needs to end in your life? What will open up when it does?

14—TEMPERANCE

Temperance offers a restful haven amid intense cards like Death, the Devil, and the Tower. The landscape here is peaceful, with a clear pond and blooming irises. It is graced by the presence of an angel. The road ahead can wait for a while.

The angel has massive red wings and a shining halo, but he's rolled up the sleeves of his gown in a very human way. His hands are strong and capable, pouring water back and forth between two golden goblets at an impossible angle. He's perfectly poised, with one foot on land and one in the cool water.

Everything here is balanced and flowing. You can dip your toe in the water without throwing yourself in. You don't have to choose one cup over the other. There is time to heal, to consider options, and to find solutions.

- *Card interpretation:* Temperance advises balance and moderation in all things. Going to extremes won't support your well-being. Meet yourself where you are. Pay attention to your energy levels and modulate your behavior to support what flows best. Instead of drastically cutting something out or doubling down on something else, seek the middle ground. That is where you'll find your flow. When it comes to challenging situations, a diplomatic approach will bring resolution. Ultimatums halt dialog and stifle ideas. You'll discover innovative solutions by calmly exploring options and inviting give-and-take.

- *Talisman intention themes:* Work/life balance, scientific or artistic pursuits, finding solutions, energetic equilibrium, moderation in habits or behavior.

- *Affirmation:* I understand my energy patterns and flow in harmony with them.

- *Musings:* What is flowing well for you? Where are you forcing things or working against your natural flow of energy?

15—THE DEVIL

In a dark imitation of the Lovers card, the Devil looms over two naked people chained to his stone perch. But the heavy chains are hung loosely around their necks. They could lift them off and walk away. But would they dare to do that with the Devil looking on?

The Devil also mocks the Magician card, telling you that you have no power of your own. Instead of raising a wand to the heavens as the Magician does, the Devil points his torch to the ground. An inverted pentagram replaces the Magician's infinity sign, symbolizing the domination of matter over spirit and the Devil's separation from the light.

The Devil tells you that you're powerless to make changes in your life. He controls through illusion, throwing your darkest fears and secret shame at you. He wants you to believe that you've sunk too low to rise, that you're worthless and broken. He wants to convince you that it's better to do nothing and stay in this dark place, even though it feels like hell.

- *Card interpretation:* It's time to remove those chains. You may feel trapped by an unhappy or harmful situation, relationship, or behavior, but you're not as powerless as you imagine. Fear, fatigue, or negative influences tell you that you're incapable of changing your circumstances, but that's not true. It takes courage to acknowledge where you are and how you got there. And it may seem easier to stay with what's familiar. But realize that whatever that Devil represents is stealing your joy and energy. Love yourself, reclaim your power, and choose to set yourself free.

- *Talisman intention themes:* Leaving a toxic situation, freedom from addiction, facing fears, reclaiming your power.

- *Affirmation:* I have the power to free myself from negative influences.

- *Musings:* How are you holding yourself back? What stories are you telling yourself that aren't true?

16—THE TOWER

Chaos. Two people plummet headlong through the black sky, having thrown themselves out of a burning tower to escape the destruction. Their hands grasp at the air, and their eyes are wide with shock and helplessness. Whatever it was, they didn't see it coming.

This card's central figure is a tower perched on a craggy mountain peak, too high in the clouds for stability or comfort. It was built on shaky ground, so its fall was inevitable, but a bolt of lightning has helped events along. The lightning knocks a golden crown off the top of the tower, representing a revelation that is a significant blow to the ego.

THE TOWER.

- *Card interpretation:* We've all had a Tower moment. We think we're going along just fine, even feeling as if we're on top of the world. Then everything blows up around us. Or we may blow it up ourselves when the pressure of a particular situation becomes too much to contain. The Tower appears in times of disruption and upheaval—times when your world turns upside down and what you thought you could count on crumbles around you. A sudden blast of clarity that changes everything often precedes this event. It is destabilizing, to say the least. But believe it or not, the Tower sets you free. Rather than being trapped under the rubble of something that wasn't working, you're released. When the dust settles, you can rebuild your life on a much stronger foundation. Trust in your resilience and take pleasure in a fresh start on your own terms.

- *Talisman intention themes:* Releasing pressure, rebuilding after disaster or shock, liberation.

- *Affirmation:* Nothing keeps me down.

- *Musings:* What kind of freedom is the Tower offering you? Can you release some pressure, or do you need to let the Tower explode?

17—THE STAR

The Star invites you to make a secret wish, trusting in your heart that it will come true. After the darkness of the Devil and the devastation of the Tower, the light of the Star guides you to a peaceful place where your faith is restored, hope lives, and healing begins.

The Star is naked; she shines, concealing nothing. Kneeling on soft, green grass beside a pond and surrounded by a starry sky, she holds a pitcher in each hand. She pours water onto the land from one and back into the pond from the other. One of her feet rests on the land, while the other rests on the pond's surface in a quietly miraculous way. She's perfectly balanced. She's focused on her pouring, and the flow of water is generous and limitless. Perched in a nearby tree, an ibis watches over her—a bird sacred to Thoth, the Egyptian god of wisdom, writing, and magic. Its song is filled with wise messages and uplifting guidance.

- *Card interpretation:* The Star appears with a message of hope. All will be well. You've gone through experiences that have tested your faith and made you question yourself. But now you can breathe and rest and start to heal. You're on the right path, but there's no hurry to get moving yet. Throughout those challenging times, you discovered who you are. The layers you wore to protect or hide or please others have fallen away, along with the limitations they caused. Now you know your strength, your resilience, your unique gifts. Part of the healing process is to live as yourself, in all your glory, knowing that you have nothing to prove. When you're ready, shine like the star you are.

- *Talisman intention themes:* Healing, energy work, hope, wish come true, living as your true self.

- *Affirmation:* I am the star of my own life.

- *Musings:* What gives you hope? When has a dream come true for you?

18—The Moon

The Moon stirs up deep fears and hidden longings, and reminds you that thrilling mysteries await you in the dark. The scene on this card is unsettling and strange, without any human figures apparent. Drawn by the moon's gravitational pull, a spiny crustacean crawls out of a pool, unsure if it will fully emerge or sink back into the depths. Two canine creatures stand on either side of the pathway, howling at the moon. Is one a dog and one a wolf? It's impossible to tell friend from foe in the moonlight. The face of the moon above is impassive, its eyes closed.

The creatures on the card represent aspects of your psyche. The crustacean drags up emotions you've relegated to the depths of your subconscious; it's trying to get your attention. The dog is the part of you that needs love, companionship, and approval; the wolf reminds you that you are wild and wise. You know you need to continue your journey, but even with the moonlight to guide you, the path ahead is shadowy and winding. Since you can't rely on your mundane senses to show you the way, you must gather your courage, trust your intuition, and tread carefully.

- *Card interpretation:* The Moon card offers illusion and confusion, but you have resources to support you. Trust your intuition, pay attention to your dreams, and look beneath the surface of all situations. You have strong instincts. Let them point you in the right direction. If you're feeling anxious about the future, bring your fears into the light and examine them. When you let them swim around in your subconscious, vague and undefined, they may seem more daunting than they really are. Don't be afraid to go into your shadows; you'll find insight and healing there. This card invites you to honor your phases and cycles, and the ebb and flow of your energy. You'll experience times of waxing, attaining fullness, and waning throughout your life, just as the moon does. Just live in the mysteries rather than trying to control them.

- *Talisman intention themes:* Shadow work, facing your fears, connecting with Divine Feminine energy, trusting your intuition, psychic practices.

- *Affirmation:* I am as wise, mysterious, and multifaceted as the moon.

- *Musings:* Do you remember your dreams? What messages have they been sending you recently?

19—The Sun

The Sun greets you with pure joy. Its rays pulse and fill the sky, extending beyond the boundaries of the card. Sunflowers peek over the garden wall, stretching toward the sun's life-giving energy. Seated on a gentle horse, a golden-haired child throws its arms open wide, receiving all the blessings the sun offers, while reaching out to embrace the world.

The child waves a red banner, because getting to this point in the cards and in life is a victory to celebrate. The red feather that it wears has been on a journey as well. We saw it at full strength with the Fool, then withered away with Death. Now it returns to its full vigor.

The garden is paradise, but freedom and adventure are calling, so the horse and child leap over the wall to experience more of life. We follow them and ride triumphantly toward the culmination of the Major Arcana—to the journey's end—yet everything feels new.

- *Card interpretation:* The sun is shining on you, and life is good. Enjoy these golden days. You've navigated shadows to get here, and now the world is bright and clear. Surrender to joy and trust that it will last. You deserve all the miracles and marvels that come your way. Open your heart and receive them without reservation. Embrace your life with childlike delight, trust, and anticipation of fun. This card also brings a message of success. You're being seen and appreciated for your accomplishments, so receive accolades with gratitude, confident that you are worthy. Now is not the time to be humble or stay behind the scenes. Enjoy the spotlight and shine bright.

- *Talisman intention themes:* Success, recognition, inviting in joy, worthiness, healing your inner child.

- *Affirmation:* I radiate joy and draw blessings to me.

- *Musings:* What do you love about your life? What made you smile today?

20—JUDGEMENT

At this point in the Major Arcana, you are close to the end of the journey. But you must face Judgement Day before you can successfully complete it.

The word "judgement" carries negative connotations. No one likes to be judged for their behavior, especially if they fear they may be found lacking. But in the Judgement card, the reckoning has already occurred, and everyone present has come through with flying colors. The archangel Gabriel blows his trumpet, a sound you can't ignore. The dead joyfully rise from their graves with arms stretched wide in wonder and praise for the angel. They are free and ready to be reborn.

- **Card interpretation:** The Judgement card is a wake-up call on a cosmic scale. It's a revelation you can't ignore—a blast of clarity that stops you in your tracks. Everything in your life has led to this. You hear your calling and understand your purpose, and it's time to live in alignment with it. This card appears when you're on the cusp of transformation. You've been playing small, holding yourself back out of fear or lack of confidence. But you've been preparing yourself for this metamorphosis and are now ready to break free and rise to the challenge. Let go of judgements you've placed on yourself. Draw a line under the past and move into a new, authentic, expansive phase of life. There's no turning back now.

- **Talisman intention themes:** Following your calling, knowing your purpose, breaking free of limitations, letting go of the past, transformation, rebirth, rising up.

- **Affirmation:** I rise to the challenge and answer my calling.

- **Musings:** Are you judging yourself too harshly? What can you release from your past?

21—THE WORLD

This card may remind you of the Wheel of Fortune, which depicts a similar scene. But while the Wheel of Fortune stands about halfway through the Major Arcana and gives only a glimpse of the mysteries of life, the World reveals all.

A woman floats in the blue sky in a fluid pose. From this bird's-eye perspective, she takes one last look at the past, while preparing to step forward into the next phase of life. The laurel wreath surrounding her announces that she has reached the triumphant culmination of a long journey. The ribbons at the top and bottom of the wreath form a lemniscate, or infinity symbol, indicating that the world never ends and that life is eternal. The woman is balanced and whole, with two magic wands in her hands.

The four creatures in the corners of the card represent the four fixed signs of the Zodiac, the four elements, and the four directions. These situate the woman; she knows where she is in the world. She has manifested the reality she desired, and now she's about to begin again—this time with both the optimism and faith of the Fool and the wisdom of the World.

- *Card interpretation:* You are glorious. Your path was long, and you had moments of self-doubt along the way. But now you've reached heights you never dreamed possible. Pause and appreciate your accomplishments. Take a moment to reflect on how you got here and everything you learned about yourself on your journey. You're stronger and wiser than when you began and you know yourself well. A cycle of your life, or a significant situation within it, has reached its successful completion, and another is about to begin. Free yourself from loose ends or energetic ties that hold you back, because you're about to level up, move forward, and start a new adventure.

- *Talisman intention themes:* Completion, achieving success, attaining closure, moving into a new phase of life, gaining wisdom, traveling.

- *Affirmation:* I am transforming into a higher version of myself.

- *Musings:* Do you celebrate your accomplishments? Do you reflect on the past before you move forward?

CHAPTER 4

The Minor Arcana

While the Major Arcana represents significant milestones, life lessons, and spiritual revelations, the Minor Arcana depicts daily life with all its joys and challenges. These cards reflect day-to-day matters that are more in our power to control than the milestones seen in the Major Arcana—but that doesn't make them any less meaningful. We live much of the human experience in these moments. These are the times when we try our best, manage practical pressures, enjoy simple pleasures, and care for the people we love.

In a traditional deck, there are fifty-six Minor Arcana cards, divided into four suits—Wands, Cups, Swords, and Pentacles. As you learned in chapter 2, each suit is comprised of cards numbered from Ace to Ten, plus four Court Cards called Page, Knight, Queen, and King. Each of these suits governs a particular area of life and is associated with an element to help you understand its themes and guidance. Wands are linked to Fire; Cups are linked to Water; Swords are linked to Air; Pentacles are linked to Earth.

In this chapter, we'll explore each suit's characteristics and the meaning of each card's number or rank. Then we'll look more deeply into the scenes on the cards, which are like vignettes from a movie or a play that invite you to dive in and find yourself in the story that's playing out. Often, the key to understanding the messages of these cards lies in recognizing who you are in the card and what you are doing. As with the Major Arcana, I offer my interpretations of these based on my own experience, but I urge you to take my comments as a starting point and create your own connections, meanings, and stories. You'll use these interpretations when you begin to craft your talisman. Once again, I include interpretations, themes, and affirmations for each card, as well as musings to encourage reflection. Let's start with Wands.

Wands

Wands are your spirit. They represent passion, creativity, ambition, and the desire to expand. With its association with Fire, this suit is the spark that lights you up and inspires you to burn bright and fully engage with life.

Ace of Wands

The Ace of Wands is a flash of divine inspiration that sends you a brilliant idea or opportunity, as well as the means to achieve it. A hand miraculously emerges from a cloud, offering you a magic wand. Don't hesitate; grab on to it and let the sparks fly! You feel the giddiness of possibility in your soul and the excitement of a new passion, so feed those flames rather than smothering them with doubts, caution, or limited thinking. Let go of unnecessary limitations or fears.

ACE OF WANDS.

Aces are pure potential that can only be realized when you take action. With the Ace of Wands, you have the potential to engage more fully with life, express your creativity, and achieve your desires. Be bold and take the first step in that direction; this is a sign that it's your time to set the world on fire.

- *Talisman intention themes:* Starting an exciting new project, embarking on a passionate romance, leadership, creativity, ambition.

- *Affirmation:* I take divinely inspired action.

- *Musings:* What are you excited about? If you had a magic wand in your hand, what would you do with it?

Two of Wands

You've got the whole world resting comfortably in your hand, yet you're looking over the horizon thinking: "What's next?" Perhaps comfortable isn't for you; your fiery ambition tells you there are more adventures and achievements out there that are worth striving for. And they are calling to you now.

The wand behind you in the scene is bolted securely to the wall. Something you have already created is solid and has your back. The wand you are holding in front of you draws your attention. It's a new venture ready to expand. Which one will you focus on? Or is there room for both? Before you make your move, spend some time daydreaming and creating a vision for the future. Decide how much you are willing to risk and how far you are willing to go. Challenge yourself to release limiting beliefs. Prepare and let your excitement build until you have clarity around your intentions.

- **Talisman intention themes:** Expanding business or career, traveling, working or living internationally, creating the world you desire, confidence.

- **Affirmation:** I have the resources I need to fulfill my dreams.

- **Musings:** What kind of world do you want to create for yourself? What is your wildest dream?

Three of Wands

Your ships are coming in, and the world lies at your feet. This success didn't come to you by chance, however. When you encountered hardships that tested your endurance, your passion and ambition carried you forward. Your dreams have taken root, and you're ready to plan your empire.

Strategy is crucial to future achievements. It may feel lonely and windswept from your high vantage point, but you need that distance and perspective to

see all the moving parts of your life and figure out how to bring them together into a solid plan. Take advantage of this chance to move to the next level, where you can enjoy less hustle and more direction. Capitalize on the situations you orchestrate.

- *Talisman intention themes:* Expansion, confidence, success, travel, creating a strategic plan.

- *Affirmation:* I am passionate about my strategy for future success.

- *Musings:* Do you look to the future with excitement, or with trepidation? If it's the latter, how can you increase your confidence?

Four of Wands

The Four of Wands is your invitation to join the celebration. This card is such a joyful scene that you want to jump right into it. Whatever the occasion, you are welcome—a wedding, a family birthday, the return of happy days, or a party honoring a shared achievement. No formal occasion is required—you can create a reason to gather and have fun with family and friends. Aside from celebrations, this card promises harmonious family life. If you're planning a visit or a move back home, you will be greeted with love and support.

The Four of Wands also illustrates the importance of community and sharing the company of kindred spirits, whether in your workplace or while pursuing interests and passions. If you crave meaningful connection, seek it; it's out there waiting for you.

Fours in the tarot indicate stability. But because the Four of Wands is connected with the element of Fire, it shows that you can create a kind of stability in your life that is flexible and open, and that accommodates everyone.

- *Talisman intention themes:* Creating community, joy, celebration, wedding or family occasion, fun with friends, happy home life.

- *Affirmation:* I always find time and reasons to celebrate.

- *Musings:* When was the last time you enjoyed a party or celebration? What was the best part of it?

Five of Wands

There's a lot of passion and excitement in the Five of Wands, but no direction or collaboration. It looks as if the figures on the card are attempting to build something, but they each have their own idea of how best to do it. Or are they playing a game in the spirit of friendly competition? Either way, the atmosphere is supercharged, chaotic, and likely to give you a headache.

The sparring and jostling for position you see here may reflect a group dynamic you're currently experiencing. There's no point in trying to sort things out; decide whether to extricate yourself or dive in. The challenge may do you good, and there's no harm in occasionally shaking things up and pushing boundaries. You'll fire up your creativity and have the chance to release any pent-up energy and frustration.

The Five of Wands also appears when there is conflict within yourself. Is there an issue that you're trying to sort out? Or a creative project that is giving you problems? Rather than looking for a logical resolution to this tension, explore your feelings and give them some form of healthy expression. This messy energy is part of the process.

- *Talisman intention themes:* Firing up creative energy, stirring up a stagnant situation, competition, sports or team activities, rivalry.

- *Affirmation:* I'm up for a challenge.

- *Musings:* Are you a competitive person? Does competition bring out the best or the worst in you?

Six of Wands

The Six of Wands is often called "the victory card." A triumphant figure on a horse, crowned with a laurel wreath, dominates the scene. In the background, you can see a procession of people on foot, cheering the rider onward. So even though everyone is celebrating a victory, there are still more battles to be won.

Like the central figure on the card, you're riding high, heading toward success. It takes courage to rise above the crowd and claim a commanding role, but you're ready to answer the call to leadership. You have so much charisma right now, and your passion is irresistible. Use that energy to inspire others and provide them with much-needed direction. Aside from the benefit you will gain, you can use this opportunity to showcase your talents and achievements, and build a loyal following.

If you're facing a challenge and secretly doubt your ability to overcome it, let other people cheer you on. Borrow confidence from your admirers and the people rooting for your success.

- *Talisman intention themes:* Leadership, victory, creating a following for yourself, confidence.

- *Affirmation:* I am a confident and capable leader.

- *Musings:* Do you acknowledge and celebrate your victories? Are you too humble?

Seven of Wands

I imagine the people using the six wands shown in this scene to be menacing the figure on the hill. Clearly, he was ambushed. He only had time to throw on a mismatched shoe and boot, grab the seventh wand, and brace himself against attack.

When the Seven of Wands appears, you are in a situation where you must stand up for yourself and defend your territory. You're on top, and it took grit and effort to get there. Now there are people around you who would love to knock you down and take your place. Others demand your time and attention, and question your beliefs. They are attempting to push past your boundaries. It's too much. You can't pick your battles or play nice. You just have to give a big "no" to everyone and everything.

You are using all your energy to fend off attacks and protect yourself, which is frustrating, because you have other goals you'd rather be pursuing. But there's no room for creating success until you have dealt with these challenges to your position.

- *Talisman intention themes:* Determination, defending your territory, fending off attackers, fighting spirit, upholding boundaries and beliefs.

- *Affirmation:* I stand up for myself.

- *Musings:* When was the last time that someone pushed you too far? How did you deal with the situation?

Eight of Wands

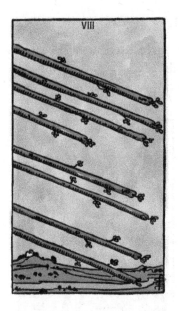

The Eight of Wands is one of the only cards in the deck that depicts no human beings, animals, or magical creatures. In the scene, the wands fly so fast across the countryside toward their target that nothing can keep up. That's for the best, because the last thing you need right now is interference with your momentum.

Events are speeding up, and all forces are aligned. So get out of your own way and let them unfold. It won't do any good to stand in front of those wands and wave your arms to try to block or divert them. Instead, focus your energy on your desired outcome. It may feel scary, because what you set in motion has now taken on a life of its own. But you're so close to manifesting your goal. You're ready for success and positive change, and the good news they will bring.

- *Talisman intention themes:* Movement, speedy outcomes, sending or receiving a message, success, travel.

- *Affirmation:* I know when to get out of my own way.

- *Musings:* When you are close to achieving a desire, do you pull back or try to change course? Do you sabotage your own success? If so, what helps you to move through this resistance?

Nine of Wands

The figure on the Nine of Wands is battle-weary and vigilant. He leans heavily on his staff, looking over his shoulder and anticipating danger. He stands behind a makeshift fence of wands, which provides some protection. But it also limits his freedom and mobility. The bandage on his head is evidence of the mental strain and injury he's suffering, yet he's still standing strong and defending his position.

Just like him, you're tough. You carry scars from past betrayals and defeats, but each one increases your determination to keep going. Even though you're bone-tired, you know you can't relax your vigilance—yet. You are close to the end of this struggle, and you have the strength to hold on a little longer. Continue to guard your interests and protect yourself until the threat has passed and you have triumphed. Don't give up now.

- *Talisman intention themes:* Determination, resilience, strength, protecting yourself and your property, resources or business, making a last stand.

- *Affirmation:* I have the strength to see this through.

- *Musings:* What inspires you to keep going when stretched to your limit? What will you protect at all costs?

Ten of Wands

You are in the home stretch. But you can't see it, because you're focused on the burden you're awkwardly lugging. Although it would be easier to drop some of the wands you're carrying, you'd never do that, because you're passionate about what each one represents to you and determined not to leave

any behind. Your desire for new experiences and your reluctance to turn down a challenge have put you in this position. Now you must call on all your resolve and push through to the end. It won't be easy, but it will be satisfying.

Once you've achieved your goals and arrived at that sweet little house we can see on the card, remember to lay down your wands and rest. They may feel like a part of your body and soul, but don't continue carrying them once you have fulfilled your responsibility. And in the future, before you take on too much, ask yourself if this is something you really want or need to do. Is it something you have to take on alone?

- *Talisman intention themes:* Successful completion of a task or project or journey, getting back home, stamina, determination, reaching a goal on your own.

- *Affirmation:* I work smarter, not harder.

- *Musings:* Do you tend to take on too much? When you're overwhelmed, do you ask for help, or push through on your own?

Page of Wands

The Page of Wands is an adventurer. He has the same enthusiasm and openness as the Fool, and you may recognize the same red feather in his hat. But unlike the Fool, he is prepared for the journey ahead. He has a tall walking stick, a warm cloak, a hat and sturdy boots, and a plan to experience as much of the world as possible.

This Page is a bright spark who easily charms others into joining his adventures, wild schemes, and mischief. He isn't concerned about getting into trouble. He knows he can talk his way out of any sticky situation, and his curiosity always takes precedence over caution.

When the Page of Wands appears in your cards, approach life with his spirit of adventure. Be fearless; try something new; discover what drives your passion. You may get into some scrapes, but it's worth it as long as you're having fun.

PAGE OF WANDS.

- *Talisman intention themes:* Starting a new adventure, traveling, having fun, discovering your passions, feeling like a kid.

- *Affirmation:* I am delighted and amazed by my life.

- *Musings:* Are you ready for an adventure? What are you excited to discover about yourself?

Knight of Wands

The Knight of Wands is a firebrand. He is driven by passion, and his presence heats up every situation. He stirs up desire, outrage, and rebellion in the hearts of previously sensible and mild-mannered people. When he rides off to pursue new heroic exploits—as he always does—he leaves behind a trail of broken hearts and wild tales.

This fiery Knight can be arrogant and impulsive, but he's an idealist at heart who is happiest when helping the powerless or bringing down an oppressor. Give him one clear-cut quest or task, and he won't rest until he's fulfilled it. He craves action, creates change, and is never boring.

KNIGHT OF WANDS.

When the Knight of Wands appears, he invites you to be dashing and fearless. Go after what you want quickly and precisely, focusing on short-term goals and fast results. Don't worry too much about the future. What you do in this present moment is what matters. Let yourself get caught up in your own heroic story.

- *Talisman intention themes:* Fighting for a cause, engaging with life, confidence, increased vitality, feeding your passion, romance, purpose, adventure.

- *Affirmation:* I stir things up and spark change.

- *Musings:* What are you passionate about? Who or what makes you feel as if you could conquer the world?

Queen of Wands

The Queen of Wands is a witch, accompanied by her black cat. Unlike the other Queens in the tarot, she sits on her lion-adorned throne with knees spread wide, confidently claiming her space. The other members of the Wands family live in dry, desert landscapes surrounded by salamanders. But the Queen holds

QUEEN OF WANDS.

a blooming sunflower, and greenery decorates her crown. She is unique, full of life, and blazing with creative fire.

This Queen fascinates everyone she meets. She has the temperament of a passionate artist, an entrepreneurial visionary, an actor, and a storyteller with a wicked sense of humor. She sees the world differently than most, and looks to the future with optimism and self-assurance.

When the Queen of Wands appears in your cards, tap into the fiery, feline side of yourself. Take pleasure in who you are; appreciate your intelligence and wit, and your unique way of expressing yourself. Don't worry too much about what other people think about you. Choose the unconventional path that lights you up and makes good use of your talents, rather than trying to fit into someone else's world.

- *Talisman intention themes:* Creativity, self-confidence, magic, witch-craft, acting, artistic or entrepreneurial pursuits, passion, self-love, worthiness.

- *Affirmation:* I am a passionate and creative being.

- *Musings:* How do you express your creativity in your daily life? What do you see differently from most people?

King of Wands

The King of Wands is a fiery leader. He finds it challenging to sit still on his throne. He'd rather leap up and head off on an adventure like a Page or a Knight, but he has the presence of mind to conquer his impatience and cares too deeply about his responsibilities to toss them aside. Because of his abundance of confidence, he is often overbearing, and his clenched fist and intense stare reveal a struggle to control his hot temper.

KING OF WANDS.

The tension between ideas and action defines this King. He is a visionary who sees patterns and trends quickly, and is able to come up with innovative strategies for future success. But ideas aren't enough for him. He understands that a vision is only a daydream if you don't take action to manifest it in the world.

When the King of Wands appears, channel your passion into a productive form, rather than letting it devolve into burnout or frustration. Find the courage and confidence to propose ideas no one else could conceive. When looking to the future, first create a flexible strategy, then pursue your burning ambitions with all you've got.

- *Talisman intention themes:* Leadership, creating a strategy for the future, ambition, confidence, power, success in career or business.

- *Affirmation:* I manifest my vision.

- *Musings:* What is your vision for the future? What steps do you need to take to make it happen?

CUPS

The Cups are your heart. They represent your emotions, your intuition, and your compassion, and anything you love. This suit inspires you to fall in love, to get your heart broken, and to follow impossible dreams. Like water, Cups replenish you and keep you flowing.

Ace of Cups

This golden cup is your personal Holy Grail, something you long for and search for—a seemingly impossible quest. Yet here it is now, a miracle resting gently in your hand. A hand appears from a cloud, offering you your heart's desire.

Receive it with joy and thanks, knowing it's meant for you and that you're worthy of it.

The Ace of Cups overflows with love. It may bring a romantic relationship full of potential or a new approach to love. A baby may be on the way; a wounded heart may start to heal. A dove places a communion wafer in the cup, bringing peace and reminding you of the loving presence of the Divine within you. When the Ace of Cups appears, it invites you to open your heart and allow it to be filled.

- *Talisman intention themes:* Love, self-love, healing, abundance, peace, fulfillment, miracles, finding your heart's desire, opening to receive blessings.

ACE OF CUPS.

- *Affirmation:* I am loved.

- *Musings:* Do you believe in miracles? Have you experienced one?

Two of Cups

The Two of Cups may represent a new romantic relationship or the rekindling of an old one—a deep friendship or a powerful meeting of kindred spirits. On this card, two people share a moment, and a significant partnership begins. They look directly into each other's eyes and, as they raise their cups, they make a promise. Their hearts are aligned, and they'll go wherever this soul connection takes them.

Although this is a very human scene, the presence of the Divine reveals the importance of what's happening here. A fierce, winged red lion hovers above the pair, blessing and protecting them. The caduceus— the god Hermes's staff around which snakes intertwine—floats between them, symbolizing balance, communication, and reciprocity.

The Two of Cups lets you know that a partnership will impact your life. This relationship's success depends on maintaining heart-to-heart communication and mutual respect. You're making yourself vulnerable by opening your heart, and so is the other person. Be generous and honest, and willing to trust.

- *Talisman intention themes:* New romance or friendship, equal partnership, connection, promises, agreements, successful negotiations.

- *Affirmation:* I value meaningful connections and mutual respect.

- *Musings:* What do you value most in a partnership? What do you expect from a partner, and what are you willing to offer?

Three of Cups

Three friends dance in a circle, raising their glasses in celebration. They are so close and comfortable with each other that it's difficult to see exactly where one starts and another ends. The dancers are surrounded by lush grapes and ripe fruit, and have vine leaves in their hair. You know this party will get wild. Magic happens when dear friends gather to celebrate life and each other.

When the Three of Cups appears, spend time with close friends who know you well and love you just as you are. Call in your circle of friends when you need support. Get together to blow off steam, enjoy each other's company, and have a good laugh at how messy life can be. True friends and soulmates are precious resources. When they share your life experiences and wisdom, it is a tonic for your heart.

- *Talisman intention themes:* Friendship, community, kindred spirits, witchcraft, celebration, dance and movement, collaboration, support.

- *Affirmation:* I nurture my friendships.

- *Musings:* What qualities do you admire in your dearest friends? What do you think they appreciate about you?

Four of Cups

The figure on the Four of Cups is the embodiment of passive resistance. As on the Ace of Cups, a wondrous hand reaches out of a cloud to offer a golden cup to a person seated under a tree. But this person sits with arms crossed and eyes down, refusing to look at what is being offered. Why?

Perhaps the cup contains something unwanted—the same old stuff as in the three untouched cups lined up in front of the figure. It may be wise to resist repeating a pattern that no longer serves. But the cup being offered may hold a magic potion or represent an amazing opportunity. Yet the figure seated under the tree appears overwhelmed with ennui, detached from surroundings, and too stubborn to look at what's being presented.

If you're feeling bored or unsatisfied, it may be time to break behavior patterns that keep you stuck in a rut. The Four of Cups suggests that you consider your choices well; don't repeat unproductive or negative patterns out of apathy. And if there is the prospect of greater fulfillment right in front of you, reach out and grab it. Remember that Cups are connected to the heart, so this advice applies especially to offers that are presented to you with love, concern, or admiration.

- *Talisman intention themes:* Making good choices, engaging with life, meditation, mindfulness, breaking negative patterns, recognizing opportunities.

- *Affirmation:* I recognize and act on advantageous opportunities.

- *Musings:* Have your interests changed? Does what used to please you now leave you cold?

Five of Cups

Draped in a black cloak, a figure mourns. The three spilled cups and the sadness they represent consume his attention. He has lost someone or something, or life didn't go as he hoped. Two shiny upright cups stand at the ready behind him, filled with the promise of happier times ahead, but he isn't ready to see them.

The Five of Cups calls to mind many idioms. There's no use crying over spilled milk. It's water under the bridge. Cross over the bridge to the other side. Everything in the card wants to move this grieving person forward. However, it would be insensitive and pointless to tell someone who drew this card in a reading just to cheer up.

If you're grieving, do it at your own pace and in your own way. Grief is a process. You don't want to stay in this place of immobilizing sadness forever, but allow yourself time to feel, to digest, and to forgive. Give yourself a chance to understand how your life has changed. When you're ready, throw off that black cloak and prepare yourself to be happy again.

- *Talisman intention themes:* Coping with loss, managing grief, self-care, finding happiness after loss, forgiveness.

- *Affirmation:* I am healing from this loss.

- *Musings:* How have you managed loss and grief in the past? Which self-care strategies were the most helpful?

Six of Cups

The Six of Cups depicts a sweet scene in which two children stand in the courtyard of a castle or manor. One child gives the other a cup filled with white flowers, and she smiles in thanks. We know they are safe and at home, protected by a tall tower and a man carrying a staff in the distance.

This card reminds me of a fairytale or a fantasy; it doesn't look quite real. The perspective is strange. One child is bigger than the other, and their hoods and mittens are incongruous with the scene. This card is like a fond childhood memory, filled with more nostalgia than accuracy.

When this card appears in your reading, you may be longing to return to a simpler time, looking at the past through rose-colored glasses. Enjoy happy memories, or allow yourself some bittersweet melancholy without getting lost in it. Remember that life in the here and now has its blessings, too. It may be time to call a friend you haven't talked to in ages, or someone from the past may turn up unexpectedly.

On another note, the surprisingly complex Six of Cups may represent past-life exploration or ancestors who are ready to support you and work with you. It may even indicate meeting a new romantic partner you feel as if you've known all your life.

- *Talisman intention themes:* Nostalgia, childhood memories, friendship, companionship, love, ancestor work, past lives, healing your inner child.

- *Affirmation:* My memories help me understand and appreciate my present.

- *Musings:* Do you have a memory you return to when you need comfort or peace? What is it, and why does it soothe you?

Seven of Cups

Although we can't see its face, I imagine the figure on the Seven of Cups standing with eyes wide and mouth open in astonishment. This person stands in the dark, head in the clouds, confronted with seven floating cups filled with mysterious contents. Which one to choose? The victory wreath or the jewels? A castle, a dragon, or a snake? Is that a curly-haired angel? And what does the white veil conceal? How can you tell which one is the right one?

When you have a lot of options, it's easy to fall into daydreaming and pro-crastination. Once you make your choice, all the other options disappear. So

rather than risking a poor decision, it's much more fun to imagine possibilities. And if you aren't clear on what you want, it's tough to recognize it.

The Seven of Cups invites you to day-dream and let your fantasies inspire you. But the next step is to get clear on what is avail-able to you so that you can make a discerning choice. Be aware of how emotions cloud your judgment, and ask yourself if fear or self-doubt are preventing you from moving forward.

- *Talisman intention themes:* Making a choice, finding direction, clarity, fantasy, imagination.

- *Affirmation:* I turn my daydreams into reality.

- *Musings:* Think of a time when you got stuck in procrastination mode. Why did that happen, and what did you do about it?

Eight of Cups

The Eight of Cups guides you outside of your comfort zone. You've made the difficult decision to leave behind someone or something you care about and follow your path into the unknown. Wearing red boots and cloak and holding a sturdy walking stick, you head toward something about which you're passion-ate. Nevertheless, the road is dark and treacherous, and you can't help feeling melancholy. The impassive Full Moon, or perhaps a solar eclipse, illuminates your way, but doesn't reveal all.

This card indicates that you know it is time to move on. But it takes cour-age to pursue your dreams and turn your back on what's comfortable and known—especially when you know that you may hurt others in the process.

There's more for you—more to be discovered within yourself and out in the wider world. And that's an exciting journey you must make on your own. Take the first step.

- *Talisman intention themes:* Following your dream, spiritual journey, travel, pilgrimage, leaving a situation that no longer serves you well.

- *Affirmation:* I follow my heart into the unknown.

- *Musings:* Are you feeling restless? Where do you want to go? What do you want to experience?

Nine of Cups

The Nine of Cups is called the "wish card." If it appears in your reading, your wish will come true. No wonder the figure on the card looks so pleased with himself! The nine cups behind him are lined up like trophies. Love, contentment, and blessings surround him, and he knows the universe has his back. Arms crossed and feet flat on the floor, he is quite happy where he is and plans to stay there as long as possible.

When the Nine of Cups appears for you, revel in it and be joyfully grateful for the blessings you are experiencing. Your good fortune isn't due to luck or a twist of fate. Your wishes have come true because you followed your heart, acted with compassion and authenticity, and did the necessary work. Your journey through the Cups brought you grief, soul-searching, and loss, and yet your faith in love and your gratitude for it remained constant. Be proud of yourself, and trust that many more wishes will be granted throughout your life.

- *Talisman intention themes:* A wish granted, gratitude, faith, trust, satisfaction, pride in accomplishments, optimism.

- *Affirmation:* I am grateful for my life.

- *Musings:* When has a wish come true for you? How did it happen?

Ten of Cups

The Ten of Cups is one of the happiest cards in the deck. It expresses the joy of having a circle of loved ones with whom to share your life. A family dances under a rainbow in this happily-ever-after scene. Children play without a care in the world, while the couple gestures toward the rainbow and their little, red-roofed house. They invite us to marvel at their bliss and join in it.

Naturally, not every family moment is as picture-perfect as this one, and they don't need to be. The Ten of Cups encourages you to savor harmonious times at home, knowing that they are a product of consistent patience, forgiveness, generosity, and commitment to family and friends. Real joy comes from knowing that there are people who love you no matter what, through all the ups and downs of life, whether that's your relatives or chosen family. And it is a blessing to have the chance to love and be loved.

- *Talisman intention themes:* Family, children, relationship, marriage, happy home, domestic harmony, abundance, love.

- *Affirmation:* Love and support surround me.

- *Musings:* How do you imagine your happily-ever-after? Who is there with you?

Page of Cups

The Page of Cups is a tender-hearted dreamer. He is curious about the world and delights in the magic he sees all around him. Wearing bright, colorful clothing covered in lotus flowers, he poses as if he's on a stage; he is a natural performer who loves to please and entertain others.

PAGE OF CUPS.

A small fish pops out of this Page's cup. He isn't surprised and doesn't drop the cup or throw it away in fear. Instead, the two of them have a conversation, and the Page is charmed by what the fish has to say. He often has magical experiences like this, because he's open to them and follows the promptings of his intuition.

When the Page of Cups appears, be playful and seek joy. Believe in magic, and you'll find it. Approaching the world with the innocence and sensitivity of a child can leave you open to hurt feelings and harsh realities. Nevertheless, the goodness that you encounter in others will inspire you.

- *Talisman intention themes:* Intuition, opening your heart, receiving signs and messages from the universe, creativity, connecting with your inner child, being playful.

- *Affirmation:* I see magic all around me.

- *Musings:* When was the last time you were surprised and delighted? What made you feel that way?

Knight of Cups

The Knight of Cups is the archetypal knight in shining armor. He rides in on his elegant horse to save the day and offer his heart to you. His life is dedicated to the quest for the Holy Grail and he believes that, when he finds it, he'll achieve spiritual perfection and union with the Divine—and, above all,

KNIGHT OF CUPS.

love. This dreamy and chivalrous Knight is in love with the idea of love and will always follow his heart.

Although this Knight feels things deeply, his heart is often changeable. He gets carried away with the romance of a situation, and he doesn't always cope well with the realities of life, relationships, and love. He believes everything should be beautiful and perfect, and feels uncomfortable when affairs of the heart get messy.

When the Knight of Cups appears, he encourages you to be the hero of your own romantic fairytale. Be daring and bold; wear your heart on your sleeve; fight for love and idealistic causes even when the odds are against you. But don't allow yourself to be consumed by your own drama. Act on your desires; brooding and moodiness will get you nowhere.

- *Talisman intention themes:* Romance, adventure, following your heart, pursuing your heart's desire, love, opening your heart.

- *Affirmation:* I am the hero of my own romantic story.

- *Musings:* Do you believe in true love? Does love conquer all?

Queen of Cups

The Queen of Cups is an empath; her emotions are as deep as any ocean. She is completely at home in her element of water—the realm of feelings, intuition, and love. As she sits on her throne by the sea, the water undulates around her, drawn to her but not engulfing her. Her dress clings to her body as if it's wet or made of water. Her cup is the most elaborate in the suit, decorated with angels; it is the only cup with a cover. She can contain her emotions when she needs to.

A diviner and mystic, this Queen sees into the hearts of others, and she always has compassion for what she finds there. Her intuition tells her whether people are suffering or thriving, and indicates the kind of healing they need.

When the Queen of Cups appears in your cards, she gently invites you to be mindful of your feelings and moods. You feel the emotions of others so strongly—whether love or pain. Make sure that you don't take them on as your own. Because you understand what people are going through, you want to help them feel happier, more peaceful, or whole, even at the expense of your own well-being. Remember that you can heal people without losing yourself. Fill your own cup first.

QUEEN OF CUPS.

- *Talisman intention themes:* Psychic work, intuition, divination, healing, emotional balance, compassion.

- *Affirmation:* I honor my emotions and trust my intuition.

- *Musings:* How do you shield yourself from other people's emotions? How do you care for yourself when you're emotionally drained?

King of Cups

The King of Cups is a compassionate leader. He sits on a stone throne that bobs on the wavy ocean far from shore, but he's cool and calm. His eyes stay level with the horizon. His emotions run as deep as the sea, and they guide his decisions. But this King never lets his emotions drown him. He loves deeply and is a romantic at heart, but it isn't easy for him to express his feelings.

This King has experienced his share of love, heartbreak, sadness, and joy, and it has made him a wise and kind-hearted advisor. If you turn to him for help, he'll understand what you're going through. Rather than commiserating, he'll offer practical strategies and solid solutions to guide you through turbulent times.

When the King of Cups shows up in your cards, take a balanced and calm approach toward any heated situations. Don't let your emotions get the better of you. Avoid emotional outbursts; be kind and give people the benefit of the doubt. When your heart and mind are in balance, your life, creativity, and relationships flow.

KING OF CUPS.

- *Talisman intention themes:* Love, emotional healing, calm, balance, compassionate leadership, heart-centered goals.

- *Affirmation:* My emotions support and guide me.

- *Musings:* How do you stay calm and centered when life gets turbulent? Do you have a creative outlet for your emotions?

SWORDS

The Swords are your mind. They are your thoughts, your words, and your unwavering determination to find answers and understand how things work. This suit is the cold wind that blows away mental cobwebs, challenges your beliefs, and urges you to say what needs to be said.

Ace of Swords

On this card, a hand comes out of a cloud, offering you a shining sword topped with a crown and leaves of victory. If you accept it, you take on the challenge it offers. If you choose this path, it won't be easy, but you'll meet the challenge and attain the sense of achievement that comes from living in alignment with your purpose. The Ace of Swords demands that you act with unwavering conviction in yourself, your beliefs, and your truth. You must be so honest with yourself and others that your words cut to the quick.

This Ace brings clarity. You see the truth, understand a previously puzzling situation, and begin a new way of thinking. But the sword on the card is double-edged, so be aware that, although the insight you receive will be helpful, it will sting. Take this opportunity to say what needs to be said and clear the air. It will feel like a victory if you do.

ACE OF SWORDS.

- *Talisman intention themes:* Truth, conviction in yourself, clarity, honesty, victory, new perspective, focus.

- *Affirmation:* I speak my truth, even when it hurts.

- *Musings:* How do you react when others challenge your opinions? Which beliefs are worth fighting for?

Two of Swords

The woman on the Two of Swords wants to be alone. She needs peace and quiet to think clearly and reach the right decision, and she holds two big swords to help get that point across. Imagine how much strength it takes to balance those swords, how much focus and determination she has. She is serious about holding her ground and is clearly telling everyone to back off. Her crossed arms protect her heart, and her blindfold shields her from external influences.

The Two of Swords asks you to find the answers you need within yourself. The opinions of others, even if they are well-meaning,

can disrupt your focus and confuse you. Take the time and space you need to figure things out without getting stuck in the space where conflicting paths cross. Let your logical mind take the lead, but allow your intuition to back you up.

- *Talisman intention themes:* Boundaries, balance, holding your ground, making a decision, navigating a crossroad, protecting your energy.

- *Affirmation:* I think things through at my own pace.

- *Musings:* Have other people swayed your decisions in the past? What was the result?

Three of Swords

The Three of Swords is one of the most visceral cards in the deck. Not one, but three swords pierce a bright, red heart. Clouds fill the sky, and cold rain falls. You can feel the pain, heartbreak, and sorrow in this image. This person is suffering, and the loss is deeply personal. It will take time to make sense of what occurred and to start healing.

There is no point in trying to sugar-coat this card. It hurts. But when the Three of Swords appears for you, take a moment to appreciate your strength and resilience. You have been through a heart-rending experience but, despite all, your heart is very much alive and beating.

Swords relate to the mind and your thought patterns, so the path to healing starts there. Examine your perspective on what happened. Determine what you need to retain from it and what you can allow the rain to wash away.

- *Talisman intention themes:* Healing from heartbreak, divorce or separation, managing pain, changing harmful thought patterns, resilience.

- *Affirmation:* I learn from my pain.

- *Musings:* What did you learn from a time of heartbreak, loss, or betrayal? How did you begin to heal?

Four of Swords

On this card, a knight lies in a tomb with his hands in a position of prayer or meditation. A saintly figure sends him the blessing of peace from the stained-glass window above. If you look carefully, you can see the word "Pax" in the halo. The room is a quiet sanctuary where the knight can replenish and recuperate from the many battles he's fought. When you draw the Four of Swords, you can breathe a sigh of relief. You can hang up your swords and rest for a while.

When this card appears for you, make rest your priority. Deep sleep and, more important, a peaceful mind will bring the healing you need. Remove yourself from any ongoing conflicts and stressful situations. Right now, it's not your job to fight, or negotiate, or defend. Support yourself with practices that bring you calm—meditation, yoga, a break from social media, sleeping whenever and for however long you like, whatever replenishes you. Although your sanctuary may be only in your mind, retreat to an actual, quiet place that supports your well-being if you can. This time of respite will prepare you for any future challenges.

- *Talisman intention themes:* Rest, peace of mind, sanctuary, deep sleep, healing, meditation, avoiding conflict.

- *Affirmation:* I know when to pause and rest.

- *Musings:* Is there a place that makes you feel peaceful and rested? When was the last time you went there?

Five of Swords

On this card, a smug, smirking figure holds all the swords. Jagged clouds roll across the sky as he watches two other figures retreat from the battlefield, their heads hanging low in defeat.

When the Five of Swords appears, it's essential to ask yourself who you are in the card. If you are the central figure, you've won the fight. But it's a hollow victory. Your tactics are dishonorable. You have shown yourself as a bad winner, and you're left standing alone. If you are one of the withdrawing figures, you may not have come out on top, but you had the wisdom to walk away from a battle that wasn't worth fighting.

The Five of Swords indicates the presence of conflict, competition, or underhanded or unfair dealings, and reveals how you react to them. Do you want to win so badly that you will sacrifice your ethics and character to do so? Or are you willing to concede defeat in a fight you can't win, keeping your dignity intact?

- *Talisman intention themes:* Competition, conflict, walking away from a no-win situation, winning a fight, coming out on top, being ruthless.

- *Affirmation:* I know which fights are worth fighting.

- *Musings:* Have you ever walked away from a fight, even though you knew you were in the right? Have you ever won a battle and regretted how things played out?

Six of Swords

The Six of Swords shows three figures traveling in a boat, leaving behind choppy waters and headed for smooth sailing. One person guides the boat forward while the other two, an adult and a child wrapped in heavy cloaks, huddle together. We can't see their faces; no one is looking back. They know they are bound for a safer, brighter place, but they carry painful memories.

This card represents a time of transition. You may make the difficult decision to leave a place that once was home but now feels unsafe, unhappy, or stressful. Or you may be letting go of a relationship or a job that turned sour. Your decision may be based on the needs of family or loved ones for whom you hope to create a secure and happy life. Even if you feel sad or regretful about these changes, keep moving forward. Let others carry you when you need to rest. When you settle into your new place or situation, you will be able to make your peace and welcome happier days.

- **Talisman intention themes:** Moving to a new home, relocating to another country, transitioning, finding safety, leaving home, recovering after stress.

- **Affirmation:** I am headed in the right direction.

- **Musings:** What are you ready to leave behind? What are you moving toward?

Seven of Swords

The Seven of Swords depicts a thief sneaking off with someone else's swords. Or does it? Perhaps he's taking back what was stolen from him, or playing a trick on those unwitting soldiers off in the distance. Clearly, this trickster is getting away with something and feeling pleased with himself for his cleverness and audacity. But we're not sure if he's a villain, an underdog, or a hero.

This card indicates deception. Someone isn't being honest, but the reasons for this vary. The Seven of Swords may appear when you have an opportunity for personal gain in which risk is involved, so you must be stealthy and devious to succeed. Or it may be a warning that someone close to you isn't what they seem and is waiting for a chance to steal from you or betray you.

I've often seen the Seven of Swords come up when someone is tiptoeing around a sticky situation rather than engaging in direct conflict or having an uncomfortable or hurtful conversation with a partner or colleague. Sometimes avoidance is the wisest course of action in these cases, but not always. When the Seven of Swords indicates the imposter syndrome, it may not feel so clever. You may try staying under the radar, hoping no one notices that you don't know what you're doing. When this card sidles into your reading, ask yourself what kind of deception it reflects, and how you need to manage it.

- *Talisman intention themes:* Avoiding conflict, deception, personal gain, secret plans, taking a risk, cleverness, retrieving something that's been taken from you.

- *Affirmation:* I look out for my interests in a way that sits well with me.

- *Musings:* Have you ever had to be deceptive to get what you want? How did that play out?

Eight of Swords

On this card, a woman stands alone in a desolate landscape, far from the imposing castle in the background. She is blindfolded and bound, with a barricade of swords behind her. She appears powerless, but her feet aren't tied, so she can walk away. Or she could use the blade of one of those swords to cut herself free. The swords don't fence her in, and no one stands guard over her. She could escape this predicament in several ways, but she can't see that and surrenders to helplessness.

The Eight of Swords indicates that you have tied yourself up in knots by the way in which you are thinking about your current situation. It's uncomfortable; you feel isolated, trapped, and entangled in limiting thought patterns. It's poor consolation, I know, but you got yourself into this quandry and you can get yourself out. But first you have to change your perspective. You are not helpless, so trust that you'll find the solution you need.

- *Talisman intention themes:* Ending limiting thought patterns, freedom, getting out of an uncomfortable situation, self-reliance, empowerment.

- *Affirmation:* I can figure anything out.

- *Musings:* What limiting thoughts run through your mind in a loop? When you stop to examine them, do you find that are they true and beneficial, or a waste of your time?

Nine of Swords

The Nine of Swords indicates a long, dark night of the soul. It is like waking up from a nightmare at 3:00 AM, disoriented and anxious. Things will look better in the morning, but it's hours until sunrise.

The figure on the card sits up in bed in a pitch-black room. She cradles her head in her hands beneath nine swords that hang above like heavy, painful thoughts. These worries have likely been building for some time, and they now dominate this person's dreams and disrupt sleep.

If the Nine of Swords appears in your cards, you can take comfort in knowing that we've all been there. Worries left unchecked have a way of growing out of proportion, making a situation appear much worse than it really is. Try to bring your concerns into the light. Speak them out loud, or write them down. Talk to someone you trust. Don't lose sleep over past events you can't change or future possibilities you can't control.

- *Talisman intention themes:* Peace of mind, navigating worries and anxiety, understanding dreams and nightmares, coping with grief, mindfulness.

- *Affirmation:* I bring my fears and worries into the light.

- *Musings:* What keeps you up at night? How do you manage anxious thoughts?

Ten of Swords

There's no bargaining or reasoning with the Ten of Swords. Something has come to an unequivocal end. Whatever it is, it's over and done.

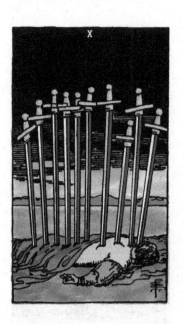

The card shows a figure lying face down by the shore, stabbed in the back ten times. He holds one hand in the gesture of a blessing, suggesting he has finally attained a state of peace. This person has nothing left to give and can't carry any more stress. Although this is a painful ending, it is necessary and a relief. We can see the first light of dawn in the distance, suggesting that the worst is over.

When you find yourself in a Ten of Swords situation, all is not lost. You've been pushed to your limit, whether you were betrayed by someone else, suffered a loss, or put yourself through hell. Now something must die so that you can be reborn. Surrender to it and know that you are on the verge of a new start, a new dawn.

- *Talisman intention themes:* Letting go, surrender, transformation, rebirth, new start, releasing pain and stress.

- *Affirmation:* I embrace necessary endings.

- *Musings:* What is ready to come to an end in your life? What space will open up when it does?

Page of Swords

The Page of Swords is a sharp student. Curious and clever, he sees the world around him as a puzzle to be solved. He wants to know how everything works and what its purpose is. "Why" is his favorite word, and he won't rest until you have answered all his questions accurately and to his satisfaction. Talking to the Page of Swords is like a breath of fresh air. He is brainy but inexperienced, so his perspective isn't clouded by preconceived ideas or outmoded ways of thinking.

PAGE OF SWORDS.

This Page needs both hands to hold up his sword. It's too big for him, and he will likely hurt himself or someone else if he tries to wield it. The same goes for his words. He is observant and wants to prove how smart he is, but he hasn't yet learned to be tactful or kind.

You may take on the role of the Page of Swords when you're a student, starting a new job, or trying something new for the first time. Allow yourself to climb a learning curve. You don't have to know everything or be perfect from the get-go. Being the star pupil is great, but mistakes and failures can be powerful teachers as well.

- *Talisman intention themes:* Studying, writing, learning something new, acquiring a skill, a beginner's mindset, thinking in a new way.

- *Affirmation:* I am a lifelong student.

- *Musings:* Is there something you've always wanted to learn how to do? What's holding you back?

Knight of Swords

KNIGHT OF SWORDS.

The Knight of Swords is an unstoppable force. The fastest moving of the tarot knights, he charges into battle like a whirlwind, with his sword drawn and his horse looking back at him in alarm. Driven by idealism, this Knight has no problem finding battles to fight and causes to defend. He always has to prove his point; he loves a good debate; he never backs down from a challenge.

With his laser-sharp mental focus, this Knight excels at achieving goals and hitting targets swiftly. His eyes remain firmly on the prize when he's on a quest. Living with this intensity, however, means that he tends to rush through life, steamrolling slower people along the way.

When the Knight of Swords appears, pursue your ambitions confidently and fight for what you believe in. Be a noble hero. But don't allow speed and tunnel vision to prevent you from seeing chances for joy, connection, and peace.

- *Talisman intention themes:* Activism, advocacy, swift results or change, fearlessness, conviction, clarity, focus.

- *Affirmation:* I achieve anything I set my mind to.

- *Musings:* What drives you? What belief do you feel is worth fighting for?

Queen of Swords

The Queen of Swords is a seeker of truth and justice. She is the toughest of the Queens and has no time for nonsense or flattery. She holds an intimidating upright sword in one hand, and she beckons you to approach with the other. When you speak to her, be honest and get straight to the point. She can see right through you, so trying to deceive her will get you nowhere. Clouds dominate the sky behind her, but she keeps her head above them. Her thoughts are clear.

QUEEN OF SWORDS.

This Queen makes decisions from her head, but isn't cold-hearted. She shares her wisdom generously and shows compassion for those who have suffered loss, pain, and bitter lessons—as she has. She has a dry sense of humor and a stinging wit, so she won't give you a hug or offer you a shoulder to cry on. But she'll tell you the truth and help you figure out your next steps forward.

The Queen of Swords invites you to speak your truth. Be honest with yourself and those around you. Trying to please, comfort, or accommodate everyone else is wearying. You know what's right and what you need to do. Don't apologize for your belief in yourself.

- *Talisman intention themes:* Empowerment, clear thinking, decision-making, speaking your truth, justice, clarity, sovereignty, boundaries.

- *Affirmation:* I know my own mind.

- *Musings:* What's more important to you—being liked or being honest? Does your answer depend on the situation?

King of Swords

The King of Swords is a logical leader. He is fascinated by people's motivations and emotional outbursts, and he can size up the dynamics of a situation in an instant. Still, he remains aloof and prefers to observe rather than join in. His detachment appears arrogant or cruel to some, but he isn't unkind. He just believes he must put aside his own emotions to rule his kingdom fairly and

KING OF SWORDS.

effectively. Don't expect empathy from him, just wise advice and hard facts.

Like the Queen, the King holds an impressive sword, but his isn't upright; it leans slightly to the side. He is willing to negotiate and discuss matters from all sides, and an air-tight argument can sway him. Although he loves a good intellectual exercise, he will never lie and his judgment is sound and fair.

When the King of Swords appears, you need to harden your heart and look at the facts of your current situation. Although you may wish that you could make a decision based on your desires, your love for someone else, or just wishful thinking, that won't serve you well in the long run, or solve any problems. Follow your moral compass this time rather than your heart.

- *Talisman intention themes:* Leadership, logic, clarity, negotiation, debate, discipline, detachment.

- *Affirmation:* I make wise decisions.

- *Musings:* When have you had to make a decision from your head rather than your heart? Was that challenging to do?

PENTACLES

The Pentacles are your body. They relate to material circumstances that contribute to your security and comfort, like your job, your home, your finances, and your physical well-being. They also speak for all the plants and creatures that live and grow in nature and enjoy the earth's abundance. This suit gives you the strength to carry your responsibilities on your shoulders, and encourages you to put down roots and enjoy the results of hard work.

Ace of Pentacles

On the Ace of Pentacles, a hand emerges from a cloud, offering you a big, gold coin. Take it; it is a gift and an opportunity to invest time, money, and resources in yourself and the life you want to create. This card may represent a new job, a new business, or a new home. It may bring unexpected financial gain or income that you have worked steadily to earn. It may also enable a new approach to your physical well-being and ease in your body. No matter what the Ace of Pentacles represents for you, it is a seed that will grow if you nurture it.

ACE OF PENTACLES.

With the promise of growth, this Ace also presents a possibility. You can stay in the lush, comfortable garden in the card's foreground and enjoy contentment, stability, and prosperity. Or you can follow the path, go through the gate, and tackle the snow-capped mountains in the distance.

When the Ace of Pentacles appears to you, there is no urgency or pressure. It is up to you to decide in your own good time if you desire the pleasures of relaxed living or would rather pursue new challenges that will push you farther.

- *Talisman intention themes:* Abundance, new job, financial gain, security, growth, well-being, comfortable home, savings, investments.

- *Affirmation:* I nurture my precious resources and my precious self.

- *Musings:* How can you invite greater abundance into your life? How can you invest in yourself and your well-being?

Two of Pentacles

The Two of Pentacles depicts a figure in the middle of a juggling act, and it will take fancy footwork to keep those coins up in the air. The juggler is managing

gracefully, but this dance requires constant focus, which is tiring and leaves little room for anything else. Even though this figure is dressed like a performer or a clown, it doesn't look as if he's having any fun; the expression on his face is one of concern or anxiety. The wavy ocean in the background shows the instability of the surrounding world, and all this person can do is roll with it for now.

The Two of Pentacles is about managing the daily demands of your life and seeking the elusive balance of work and life. Sometimes you have no choice but to juggle—taking on two jobs to pay the bills, balancing family and work responsibilities, or having two big projects going on at the same time. Your needs and well-being can get lost in that shuffle. Be mindful of the infinity symbol on this card. Have you found a flexible flow that works well for you and that is sustainable over the long run? Or are you stuck in a loop you would like to escape?

- *Talisman intention themes:* Work/life balance, managing finances or responsibilities, prioritizing, navigating uncertainty, flexibility, adaptability.

- *Affirmation:* I keep my life in balance.

- *Musings:* What are you juggling right now? What would happen if you stopped?

Three of Pentacles

The Three of Pentacles shows the power of teamwork. In this scene, three people gather in a dark, stone church. An architect refers to building plans and has the vision for the finished structure. The monk or cleric who commissioned the work looks on; the stonemason standing on a bench does the work. No one is giving orders. They are just having a conversation, sharing information and ensuring that everyone is on the same page. Each of them has a different skill, and they are all necessary to the successful completion of the final product.

The Three of Pentacles reminds you that you don't have to do it all. You're not on your own. You have valuable skills and experience that you bring to a project or enterprise, but you can rely on your colleagues to contribute their expertise. When you work with a team toward a common goal, you collectively generate energy and new ideas. You challenge each other to excel and form beneficial relationships. The whole is greater than the sum of its parts.

- *Talisman intention themes:* Teamwork, career success, networking, collaboration, building an actual structure, craftsmanship, fellowship, community.

- *Affirmation:* I value the support of a good team.

- *Musings:* In your experience, what makes a great team? How about a bad one?

Four of Pentacles

The figure on the Four of Pentacles grips four gold coins tightly. One sits on top of his crown; he holds another as a shield over his heart; his feet rest on two more. His body curls around the coins, and he's hunkered down, planning to stay right where he is. He's alone with his wealth, having turned his back on the city we can see in the distance behind him.

This card raises questions about money, security, and the use of resources. It indicates that you are in a stable financial position, while hinting that it might be a good idea to conserve your resources, save money, and beware of frivolous spending. But the Four of Pentacles also appears when you may be holding on to money or possessions too tightly, blocking the flow of prosperity out of fear or a scarcity mindset. Rather than enhancing your quality of life, focusing

on money and material things is immobilizing you. It's fine to be mindful of your finances and value the money you earn with your time and effort. But ask yourself what the point of those resources is if you don't use them to enrich your life or share your abundance with others.

- **Talisman intention themes:** Financial stability, wealth, security, savings, frugality, moderation, good spending habits.

- **Affirmation:** I manage my resources well.

- **Musings:** What is your relationship with money? Are you more comfortable spending or saving?

Five of Pentacles

The Five of Pentacles is such an unhappy scene. Two barefoot people dressed in rags trudge through the snow, determined to keep moving. The woman who leads the way hunches over in the cold; a man on crutches trails after her. The stained-glass window of a church shines behind them, but where is the door that will let them into the warmth of the sanctuary? Do they even notice the church? Or do they believe they aren't welcome there?

This card reflects financial difficulties, poverty, and despair. Perhaps you lost your job or your home, or perhaps you're struggling under the weight of debt. Until you can find a way through, you are in survival mode, and it takes stamina to keep going.

Aside from financial challenges, the Five of Pentacles may appear when you feel out in the cold, isolated, or rejected by friends, family, or community. Support on which you thought you could rely has let you down, causing a crisis of faith. But this card tells you to keep moving forward; these challenges are severe, but temporary. There are sources of help available to you, but it is hard to see them when you're overwhelmed with worry and just trying to make it through each day. Let yourself take a breath and consider options. Reach out for help when you need it.

- *Talisman intention themes:* Stamina, perseverance, finding help, faith, managing financial difficulties.

- *Affirmation:* I have gotten through hard times before and will again.

- *Musings:* How have you managed financial difficulties in the past? Were you able to find support?

Six of Pentacles

On this card, a wealthy benefactor hands out coins to two less-fortunate people who kneel at his feet. He holds balanced scales, suggesting that his generosity is fair and measured rather than overflowing. But this image evokes many questions, the most important of which is who *you* are on this card. And why do we see only one person receiving coins? Is the wealthy man holding back a few coins in his hand? Finally, is it necessary for the impoverished people to beg to receive help?

Give-and-take is a sensitive issue for a lot of us, and that is the central theme of the Six of Pentacles. When this card comes up, share your time and resources with those who need it if you're in a stable financial place. You don't need to put yourself in a precarious position to do this; carefully consider what you are able to give. If you need help to get back on your feet, ask for it and be open to receiving it. Fortunes change, and chances are you'll find yourself in both situations over the years. Allow yourself to be comfortable in each, knowing that life is a constant flow of giving and receiving.

- *Talisman intention themes:* Generosity, financial support, balance, non-profit work, justice, give-and-take.

- *Affirmation:* I give generously and receive gratefully.

- *Musings:* How do you feel when someone gives you a gift or a compliment, or offers financial support? Are you more comfortable being the giver than the receiver?

Seven of Pentacles

The gardener on the Seven of Pentacles looks tired, but he's happy to see his hard work is paying off. Things are growing. He leans on his hoe and contemplates

those seven juicy pentacles, noting which ones are ready to be harvested, what needs pruning, and where to go from here. He's watched over his crops, lost sleep over unexpected frosts and dry spells, and put up with sore muscles. He knows that growth takes time and consistent effort, and focuses on long-term results rather than rapid gain.

The Seven of Pentacles is satisfying. It shows you the tangible results of your effort, your persistence, and your skill. Pat yourself on the back and take a well-deserved rest. This is your chance to pause, to step back, and to reflect on your wider goals and plans. Are things growing as you hoped? Will you keep on doing what you're doing, or has your objective changed? What can you do to support your own growth and well-being during busy seasons? Assess your situation and muse on possibilities now, before it's too late to make changes.

- *Talisman intention themes:* Growth, hard work coming to fruition, reflection, rest, steady financial gain, long-term goals, adjustment, assessment.

- *Affirmation:* My patience, persistence, and commitment to my goals pay off.

- *Musings:* What is coming to fruition in your life? Are you pleased with the results? Is there anything you need to water, or feed, or dig up, or cut back?

Eight of Pentacles

Head down, the craftsman on the Eight of Pentacles focuses on his work. The world fades away; there is only the pentacle in front of him and the sound of his tools on metal. Even though it is repetitive work, he gets great satisfaction from it. His skill increases with each coin he makes. The finished products hang on the wall, but he pays little attention to them.

The Eight of Pentacles reflects the joy of immersing yourself in rewarding work and mastering a skill. This may be at work or at school, or when enjoying a hobby. What matters is that you are mindful of what you are doing in the moment. Stop talking about it; sit down and do the work.

If this card represents an interest or pastime, don't get ahead of yourself. Don't spend your energy planning next steps or thinking about how you can capitalize on this new expertise. Just enjoy figuring it out and learning about yourself in the process. If it represents work, take the time to do your job well. Quality is better than quantity or speed. Focus on the project at hand, and stay out of drama, office politics, or distractions.

On a practical note, you can expect to experience steady work, the same routine, and consistent income. The only changes will be within yourself—in your outlook and your increased competence.

- *Talisman intention themes:* Mastering a skill, arts and crafts, steady work, satisfying work, concentration, consistency.

- *Affirmation:* I am good at what I do.

- *Musings:* What skill have you worked hard to learn? What kept you motivated to do so?

Nine of Pentacles

The woman on the Nine of Pentacles enjoys a moment of grace, standing in her vineyard surrounded by ripe purple grapes and golden coins. One of her hands rests gently on a coin, showing appreciation for the abundant life she

created. A hunting bird perches on her other gloved hand, and she looks at it affectionately. The woman trained the bird well; it will remain still until she commands it to fly or strike. A snail glides by—a reminder of the joys of a comfortable and safe home, and of taking things slowly. The woman is alone and contented in her own company.

The Nine of Pentacles invites you to live your life well. Take a day off, surround yourself with beauty, and do what pleases you. You have worked consistently to create prosperity and financial independence. Now your challenge is to be at ease and enjoy it. There will always be work to do, and it is wise to manage your finances and career carefully. But peace of mind and well-being come from keeping a balance between hustling and relaxing. You have the self-discipline to work hard; direct that same energy toward ease and leisure. Enjoy your beautiful life.

- *Talisman intention themes:* Financial independence, abundant lifestyle, prosperity, life balance, self-discipline, self-worth, pleasure, confidence.

- *Affirmation:* I am worthy of pleasure, relaxation, and abundance.

- *Musings:* How would you spend a day off if you had one all to yourself? What do you do that's just for you?

Ten of Pentacles

Gold coins everywhere. The Ten of Pentacles represents wealth and stability, particularly in family life. In this scene, we see a family that includes a young couple, a child, two dogs, and a white-haired grandfather dressed in a mysteriously ornate robe. They are all grouped together in a grand courtyard. A veil of pentacles overlays the scene, arranged in the pattern of the Tree of Life—a reminder that magic and spirit are woven into our material world, but that often we don't see it.

It is lovely to see the enduring prosperity reflected in this card. It comes up at a time when, thanks to your efforts, life is secure and you have enough resources to live comfortably and share generously with family members who need support. But there is more to the Ten of Pentacles.

Remember that you are part of an ancestral line. You can draw support from it now, and you will add your legacy to it. What will your legacy be? What lasting wisdom, healing, or benefit will you contribute to the world? What do you want to be remembered for?

The Ten of Pentacles asks you to think long term and consider with love and care how your current actions are shaping your future.

- *Talisman intention themes:* Family, prosperity, home, ancestor work, creating a legacy, life purpose.

- *Affirmation:* My actions contribute to my abundant future and enduring legacy.

- *Musings:* What are you contributing to the world? What do you want your legacy to be?

Page of Pentacles

The Page of Pentacles is a naturalist. He loves to care for animals and tend plants and watch them grow. He instinctively understands that all creatures on earth are interconnected and support each other. He is happiest in nature, with birds and beasts for company; he is quiet and contemplative around other people. This Page often has his nose in a book, reading about practical topics

PAGE OF PENTACLES.

with hands-on applications rather than lofty philosophy. He stands in a green field holding a pentacle high with his fingertips, gazing at it with fascination and awe, determined to learn everything he can about it while keeping it safe and shining.

If you are the Page of Pentacles, what does this coin represent for you? What do you want to learn about? What resource are you ready to use? What are you ready to manifest? This may be a new job or a business prospect with the potential to increase your income and knowledge. Or it may be a course of study, or training, or an apprenticeship. This is an auspicious time to start something new and to approach it in the way the Page of Pentacles would—step by fascinated step, at your own pace, and prioritizing comprehension over hasty completion.

- *Talisman intention themes:* Study, curiosity, new job or business venture, new source of income, love of nature.

- *Affirmation:* I take my time and enjoy each moment.

- *Musings:* What fascinated you as a child? Does it still capture your imagination?

Knight of Pentacles

The Knight of Pentacles is the rock on which you can rely. The slowest and steadiest of the tarot knights, he stands quietly by, ready to help you plow through difficulties. He'll help you shoulder a burden that's too heavy for you, or offer easygoing support.

This Knight sits on a sturdy workhorse; his armor is heavy and well-used. He holds a precious pentacle and surveys his farmland, contemplating the harvest to come. He likes to have a plan and stick to it. He isn't good at changing direction once he finally gets going and, if you try to rush him, he'll dig in his heels and won't be moved.

When the Knight of Pentacles appears, trust in your strength and resilience. You have the practical knowledge and hands-on skills to manage your current situation, so don't succumb to pressure from people who want you to move faster. You know that some things need to come to fruition in their own time—including you. That being said, patience and diligence differ from stubbornness and resistance to change. So be honest with yourself to avoid getting stuck in a rut.

KNIGHT OF PENTACLES.

- *Talisman intention themes:* Stamina, strength, patience, diligence, reliability, protection, slow growth, steady work.

- *Affirmation:* I stay calm and grounded under pressure.

- *Musings:* What goal are you moving toward? Do you have a step-by-step plan to keep you on track?

Queen of Pentacles

The Queen of Pentacles is everyone's mother or cool aunt. People come to her when they need a hug, followed by calm, practical advice. She knows about life and death, and everything in between, so she always responds with compassion and without judgment.

This Queen's throne is out in lush nature. Flowers bloom around her and a rabbit hops through the scene unafraid. She holds a large, golden pentacle in her lap as she would a baby, and regards it with love. She nurtures her loved ones, but she's also highly proficient at managing a business, making money, and running a comfortable household. She's pragmatic, but she loves all the creature comforts. She knows we're meant to enjoy the pleasures of our physical world.

QUEEN OF PENTACLES.

When the Queen of Pentacles shows up for you, approach challenges with your unshakeable common sense. If you assess your current situation with a practical eye and keep your sense of humor, you can trust that you'll get it all sorted out. Your combination of compassion and capability often puts you in the role of practical caregiver, handling day-to-day arrangements and errands for loved ones who aren't up to the task. You'll never stop doing that, but look to your own self-care and nourishment as well.

- **Talisman intention themes:** Abundance, practicality, wealth, connecting with nature, running a business, managing finances, compassion, common sense.

- **Affirmation:** I create abundance and share it with those I love.

- **Musings:** What advice would you share with a younger you? What is truly worth nurturing throughout your life?

King of Pentacles

The King of Pentacles is a lavish leader. We see him seated on an ornate stone throne in his high castle. He's been sitting there contentedly for a long time—the ivy and grape vines look as if they have grown around him and fused him to his throne. The bulls' heads that decorate his throne are a nod to this King's strength, power, and stubbornness. He rests his hand on the golden pentacle on his knee; he's comfortable with his wealth and power.

KING OF PENTACLES.

This King is a shrewd businessman who understands money—how to manifest it and make it grow. He works diligently to create and maintain this abundant lifestyle, but he isn't stingy. He shares his wealth generously, knowing he can always accumulate more. He likes having company when he enjoys good food and fine wine—the best that money can buy. He is also free with his time, his experience, and his advice.

The King of Pentacles advises you to manage your resources well—including your finances, your career, your home, and your time. Maintain and protect what you have while watching for opportunities for further growth. And then dedicate some of those resources to enjoying your life. Treat yourself and your loved ones to the luxury of happy times together and a few of the finer things in life.

- *Talisman intention themes:* Wealth, business or career success, contentment, luxury, success, prestige, power.

- *Affirmation:* I enjoy sharing the finer things in life with loved ones.

- *Musings:* What does a lavish life mean to you? How would you create it?

CHAPTER 5

Reading Tarot Spreads

Now that you've gotten to know the meanings of the cards, it's time to discuss how to read them in a tarot spread.

Many tarot beginners are hesitant at first to read the cards—including myself. I devoured the little white book that came with my first deck. After that, I read all the tarot books I could find, making copious notes in an attempt to memorize all the information contained within them. When it came time to read the cards, however, I hesitated. I was afraid of making mistakes. I told myself I needed to know everything before I could perform an accurate reading, even one that was only for myself.

I was totally wrong. Tarot cards want to be read. Although they are beautiful works of art, admiring them isn't enough. Studying their fascinating scenes and symbols is time well spent, but that's only part of the magic. Their purpose is to tell stories, and we help them to do that by reading them.

In my case, the cards came to life once I got past my tendency to perfectionism and got on with reading tarot for myself and others. That leap took courage and a sense of humor. I had to give myself permission to play and look foolish. Nevertheless, I still consume as many books on tarot symbolism and mythology as I can—just for the love of it and to bring that knowledge to my readings.

A tarot reader's tools are *knowledge* and *intuition*. Knowledge comes from study and practice. Intuition comes from trust. When you bring those forces together, you see patterns, connections, and layers in the cards that reveal their story to you.

Working with the tarot is a personal practice. It's a heartfelt and honest conversation between you and the cards. You don't need to be miraculous and all-knowing. You don't have to read the cards in the same way other readers do. There isn't one right way. Find your own style and enjoy reading the cards in the way that suits you. And remember: You don't have to be perfect.

In Part II, you will work with specially designed spreads to gain insight into your intention and your talisman. Here, we'll consider what you need to know about reading the cards in order to encourage certainty, clarity, and curiosity about yourself.

YOUR TAROT RITUAL

I think that reading tarot is a ritual. There's more to tarot than the moment when you have all your cards laid out and are in the thick of interpreting them. There are things you can do to prepare for readings and steps you can take to support yourself through them. Moreover, there are routines you can follow to open and close readings that can help clarify the messages they offer. Creating a tarot ritual that incorporates these elements builds a framework that gives you confidence and helps you shift into a sacred space of heightened awareness with greater speed and ease. With each step of your ritual, you tell yourself and the universe that you are about to do something outside of the mundane world. You are about to read tarot.

That said, I don't want to discourage you from bringing out your tarot cards for a quick reading just because you don't have the time, space, or energy to perform an elaborate ceremony. Your tarot ritual can be simple, brief, and adaptable to the situation. And in time, it will become second nature.

Here are the elements I include in my own tarot ritual. Pick and choose what makes sense to you. You can add to or streamline your ritual anytime; it will evolve with your practice.

Set the Scene

Start by clearing your space, physically and energetically. Tidy up the area and clear any clutter from the table or surface where you will lay the cards. Create a comfortable place to sit that gives you the space you need in an environment conducive to a reading. That may be a quiet corner at home where you won't be disturbed, or a noisy coffee shop, or a favorite spot outside. Whatever feels right to you.

The only tools you need for a tarot reading are yourself and your cards. Still, I love to surround myself with objects that are beautiful and uplifting—a cloth to lay my cards on, a clear quartz crystal to keep the energy flowing, black tourmaline or obsidian for grounding and protection, and amethyst or labradorite for psychic awareness. If the space allows, I light a candle and include a representation of the Goddess or the deity with whom I'm working. Consider what makes you feel comfortable, uplifted, or protected, and include those elements.

Prepare Yourself

You may not see the cards clearly if you're distracted, distraught, or excited. So it's important to ground and center yourself to ensure that you go into a reading in a calm and focused state. The easiest way to do this is with a brief meditation or by just taking a few deep breaths while feeling the support of the surface on which you're sitting and the earth beneath your feet. You can also visualize a bright, white light infusing your entire body, clearing away any stagnant energy.

And now, for the most challenging part. Release any expectations you may have about yourself or the content of your reading, trusting that you'll receive the answer you need right now. The messages from the cards may be surprising and the outcome may be unanticipated, so stay curious and playful, and open to new perspectives. This provides another opportunity to remind yourself that you don't have to be perfect, bang-on, or astonishing.

Invoke Guidance and Support

An invocation is a statement that clearly states your intention for the reading. This is different from the question you want the cards to answer. In an invocation, you open your heart and share why you read tarot. You ask for the support of guides, guardians, deities, ancestors, or your higher self. An invocation is a way to connect with something bigger than yourself and access insights beyond your logical mind and life experience.

I recommend that you create an invocation you can use for all your readings—one that is profoundly personal and becomes so familiar that it flows effortlessly from your mind or lips. You can tailor your invocation to specific circumstances or occasions if needed. Here's an example of one that I use when I'm reading for myself.

> May this tarot reading be for the highest good of all concerned. May I be clear, inspired, compassionate, and grounded as I interpret the cards. I ask the elements of Air, Fire, Water, and Earth to support me; I ask spirit to guide and protect me. I am open to receiving the messages I need most and am grateful for this healing work.

Formulate Your Question

You must approach a tarot reading with a clear question you want answered. This is crucial. What is the purpose of a reading if not to answer a question? If the reason you are picking up the cards is that you have an issue or situation on your mind, ask that burning question. The more specific you are, the more specific the answer will be.

Be mindful of the language you use when formulating your question. I like to keep the tone empowering rather than fatalistic. Ask: "How can I?" Don't ask: "Will I ever?" For example, ask: "How can I invite love into my life?" Don't ask: "Will I ever find my soulmate?" The words "will I" imply that you don't have any say in the matter, that you're subject to the whims of fate. They make it appear that you can't, or don't need to, take effective action toward your goals or dreams.

But a tarot reading can inspire you with possibilities and surprise you with your own agency and capabilities. So don't give away your power. If you're facing circumstances you can't control or change, the cards can still provide you with strategies to help you navigate and understand what you're experiencing. Ask empowering questions that begin with phrases like: "How can I...?" Or: "What do I need to know about...?" Or: "What would happen if I decided to...?" Or: "What do I need to focus on...?" It can also help to include timing in your question, if that is relevant. For example: "How can I secure a fulfilling and high-paying job before the end of the year?" Or: "What if I decided to move to another country within two years?"

Take a deep breath and think seriously about what you want to know. If you don't have a specific question or are performing a daily draw, focus your intention by asking something like: "What do I need to be aware of today?" Or: "How can I make the most of today?"

And be sure to make your question about *you*. It is questionable tarot ethics to ask questions about a third party who isn't present or hasn't requested a reading. Trying to figure out what someone else is thinking, feeling, or doing won't bring clarity or peace of mind. In my experience, the cards resist questions that attempt to discern how to influence someone else's behavior or feelings toward you.

QUERENTS, SEEKERS, SITTERS, AND CLIENTS

There are several terms we use for the person who is receiving a tarot reading. A "querent" is a person who is asking a question or making an inquiry. Sometimes the terms "seeker" or "sitter" are used to refer to the person seeking answers. A professional tarot reader may prefer the term "client." If you are reading for yourself, you're the reader as well as the querent, seeker, or sitter.

Choose Your Spread

Tarot spreads give structure to your readings. The pattern in which you lay out the cards gives meaning to each position in the spread and determines how your question is answered. When read together, the meanings of those cards answer the main question that sparked your reading.

A spread can be as simple as a pattern of three cards or as extensive as a pattern of all seventy-eight cards—although I wouldn't go there personally! The spread that you choose should fit your question and be able to give you the insight you desire. It is meant to provide support, not force you to fit square pegs into round holes, so to speak. You can use traditional spreads, or you can create new spreads tailored to your situation, depending on what you want to gain from the reading. Meanings of the cards in some tried-and-true three-card spreads include: past, present, future; body, mind, soul; situation, challenge, advice; start, stop, continue; situation, advice, outcome. If none of these suit your purpose, then come up with a spread that does.

In chapter 10, I give you a tarot spread focused on clarifying the intention of your talisman. Some positions are set, but you'll have the opportunity to include a personal question as well. If you're new to tarot, use some of the simple three-card spreads given in this chapter to guide you. These can help you prepare for the more complex readings given in Part II.

Shuffle the Cards

When you're ready to start laying out the cards, shuffle them while keeping your question in mind. Any method of shuffling is fine. Just pick one that works for you and stick with it. This will add power to your readings. Following a consistent routine can encourage you to trust that the cards that come up are the right ones and leave you less open to doubts or second-guessing. It also removes the temptation to put challenging or puzzling cards back in the deck, claiming that you weren't concentrating or didn't shuffle well enough.

There are a few things to consider as you choose a shuffling method. The most important is to be gentle with your cards. A standard bridge shuffle can bend and possibly damage them. And consider whether you will keep the cards upright when you shuffle, or shuffle them in a way that may create reversals (see chapter 2). Will you shuffle and draw from the top of the deck? Or will you cut the cards and then draw? Will you shuffle until cards jump or fall out? Answering these questions beforehand can help you feel more confident in your readings.

Lay Out the Cards

I prefer to lay out all the cards in a spread face up and all at once, rather than placing them face down and revealing them one by one. I do this because I want an initial intuitive blast from the cards. I encourage you to give this a try.

Lay out all the cards face up, then take a breath and let the cards speak to you. Don't worry about the spread positions or the traditional meanings. Just notice how the cards make you feel. When you first see them, do you laugh, or smile, or grimace, or roll your eyes? Consider the mood or atmosphere of the cards. Is it happy or sad? Anxious or romantic? Hopeful, or expansive, or tired? Is it creative, or angry, or combative? Or something else? The mood will give you an idea of the theme of the reading and an indication of the answer to the question you are asking.

Notice any cards that jump out at you, as well as any symbols, colors, suits, or numbers that catch your attention. Remember: At this point, you're not interpreting the cards. You're just getting the lay of the land.

Interpret the Cards

When you've considered the potential meanings of each card, it's time to interpret them in the context of their spread position and their relevance to your question. If the position represents a challenge, for example, read it as such, even if it is a joyful card like the Sun or the Ten of Cups. If you get stuck, describe the scene you see on the card without trying to interpret it or choose the first keyword that comes to mind. You can use the interpretations in chapters 3 and 4 as a starting point.

Always listen to your intuition, even if the message you receive seems irrelevant or silly. Say the words or write them down; they may make sense in time. Pay attention to what the cards tell you; don't give your opinion. Don't fall into wishful thinking or try to fix or downplay an image that is challenging or unwanted. Trust your knowledge and your intuition. Then consult a guidebook if you need another viewpoint.

And don't be too quick to pull clarifying cards. Explore the cards in the spread fully. Suck all the information you can out of them and give yourself time to let their meanings percolate. Even if you are reading for yourself, say the meanings out loud, as if you are reading for someone else. This may initially feel strange, but it can help you avoid rushing through the cards.

WEAVING THE STORY

Now you're ready to go deeper into the spread. Remember that, as you consider the cards you laid out, you are looking for patterns and the framework of a story.

If you see a lot of Major Arcana cards, you know the question you are asking is significant. Do these cards share any themes? Is there friction between any of them? If there is only one Major Arcana card in the spread, pay special attention to it, as it carries the most weight. Let's say you are asking the cards about a potential career change, and the only Major Arcana card that appears is Judgement. Will you answer that call, knowing the momentous changes it will bring?

If you see a number of Minor Arcana cards, your question most likely revolves around everyday matters that are more under your control. Notice which suits appear. Does any suit dominate? Are the suits balanced? Are any suits missing? General topics suggested by Cups include love, relationships, emotion, intuition, and healing. Wands may indicate passion, ambition, creativity, career, and spiritual growth. Swords reflect communication, intellect, conflict, truth, and clarity. Pentacles relate to money, job, home, well-being, and resources. So a reading about a love relationship that is bristling with Swords, with Cups conspicuously absent, is clearly sending you a message.

The numbers on the Minor Arcana cards carry meaning as well. Repeated numbers emphasize a theme or stage in the story. Several Aces indicate you're at the beginning of a story, filled with potential and promise. Fives are the messy middle, while Tens reveal that you're coming to an ending. Consecutive numbers show a progression either forward or backward. And be sure to watch for numbers that are significant to you (or the person for whom you're reading). Take note of any numbers that you consider lucky or unlucky.

Symbols on the cards can also provide meaning. Make a note of any symbols that repeat in several cards and consider what their significance may be. To give you an idea, both Justice and the Six of Pentacles feature scales, indicating a need for balance. Notice if you're drawn to a particular symbol or element on a card, no matter how small. For example, you may notice the snail on the Nine of Pentacles for the first time. Are you longing to take things more slowly?

And finally, consider the directionality of the cards and note how they interact. If there are figures on the cards that face or turn away from each other, or that point at each other, or that share a similar landscape, what meaning may that hold? For example, if there are two Knights, are they charging at each other or riding off in different directions?

Finally, when you have considered all the factors given above, use all the information you have gathered or intuited to tell the story you see in the cards. Weave them together into a narrative, using their spread positions to help you. It's easy to get lost in the cards and the story, so be sure to explore tangents.

Before you close the reading, revisit the question you asked and be sure you answered it. Empower yourself (or the person you are reading for) with actions or next steps to bring about positive change or a desired outcome. When you feel that you've said all that you can at this time, pause and reevaluate. Take one last look at your spread without considering the spread positions, as you did when you started the reading. Does anything look different to you now? Do you notice any other details?

When you finish a reading, always end with thanks and gratitude and release its energy. This closure is essential. Otherwise, you may carry the energy of the reading with you and ruminate on the outcome.

MUSINGS

- Does perfectionism come into play when you read the cards? If so, how do you navigate it?

- What kinds of expectations do you have for yourself as a tarot reader? Are they supportive, or do they need to be released?

- What will you include in your tarot ritual? Will you include all the elements I described, or do certain ones resonate with you?

SAMPLE READINGS

Read through the following examples of three-card spreads, then choose the spread that appeals to you most and give it a try. I will address each reading as if you are the querent.

Situation-Advice-Outcome Spread

We'll ask a question related to talismans here, in keeping with the theme of this book: "What do I need to know about creating and working with my talisman?" For our purposes, I will address the reading to you.

- Situation: Knight of Wands

- Advice: Seven of Swords

- Outcome: Wheel of Fortune

At first glance, my eyes go right to the Seven of Swords. This card feels like a challenge or a block between the Knight of Wands and the Wheel of Fortune, which show luck and movement. The Knight is riding forward with enthusiasm and drive, while the Seven of Swords is trailing after him causing trouble. The figure on the Seven of Swords looks back at the Wheel of Fortune. Is he trying to avoid it? Or is he looking at the one upright sword that the sphinx on top of the wheel holds, longing for a lighter load than he's carrying now? This reading generally feels encouraging if you are willing to address the Seven of Swords.

Wands show that you are passionate about creating a talisman and excited about manifesting your desire. Swords, representing thoughts and the mind, indicate that you need to shift your perspective or your mindset. The Wheel of Fortune is the only Major Arcana card, giving the sense that the timing is right for you to work your magic and that luck is on your side.

What's Your Story?

The Knight of Wands tells me you are passionate about the change you want to manifest with your talisman. You're well prepared, and your enthusiasm and determination can carry you through any challenges to success. The Seven of Swords advises you to be mindful of self-doubt and avoid the imposter syndrome. These can get in the way of achieving your dreams and being honest with yourself about what you truly desire. Your talisman is just for you; you don't need to reveal its purpose or share your plans with anyone else. The Wheel of Fortune affirms that the time is right for you to embark on this magic, so trust your instincts and go for it.

Past-Future-Present Spread

In this example, we'll use the same question as before: "What do I need to know about creating and working with my talisman?"

- Past: Temperance

- Present: Strength

- Future: Nine of Cups

The atmosphere of the cards is balanced, patient, and grounded. I like the look of the Nine of Cups; the figure on the card is pleased with how the situation unfolded.

Notice the hands of the figures on the cards. The angel on the Temperance card is holding two cups and skillfully pouring water back and forth. On the Strength card, the goddess holds a lion's jaws with confidence and compassion. The figures are using their hands to manage their situations and create change. The person on the Nine of Cups has completed the work and now stands with arms crossed, enjoying the rewards of those efforts.

The infinity symbol on the Strength card jumps out at me, and I see hints of it in the other cards. Temperance pours water in the shape of that symbol, and the arms of the figure on the Nine of Cups look like one as well. Energy is flowing smoothly, and the potential of this talisman is limitless. The central figures on all three cards wear similar white tunics, telling me that this is the same person—you—as you change and develop through the past, present, and future.

The two Major Arcana cards reveal the significance of your intention and magical work. Of the Minor Arcana, only Cups appear in the spread, so your intention for your talisman is based on emotion and has the potential to bring you much happiness.

What's Your Story?
Temperance reveals that you have been considering creating a talisman and working this magic for quite a while now. You have given yourself time and space to consider possibilities, adjust, and get the balance just right. Now you're ready to take on the challenge and do the hands-on work. You need courage and strength to achieve your goal. Luckily, you have an infinite supply of both, as we see in the Strength card. Be patient and kind with yourself. You're in control of the situation, so there's no need to try to force or rush the outcome. The Nine of Cups says you can trust that your wish will come true.

Start-Stop-Continue Spread

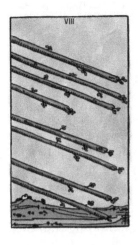  

Again, the question asked is the same as before: "What do I need to know about creating and working with my talisman?"

- Start: Eight of Wands

- Stop: Queen of Pentacles

- Continue: The Fool

The Fool makes me smile. His playful energy permeates the spread. I notice the contrast between the color schemes of the Fool and the Queen of Pentacles—the first is bright and sunny; the second is green and fertile. The Fool looks up with arms wide; the Queen looks down at the pentacle she cradles. It feels as if the cards offer the choice between those two roles or approaches.

The animals in the right-hand corners of these two cards catch my eye—the little rabbit beside the Queen and the white dog accompanying the Fool. Both are helper animals, but the rabbit is cautious and quiet, while the dog is frisky and friendly.

The Eight of Wands brings the energy of the Queen and the Fool together. The fiery wands fly with the Fool's willingness to leap into the unknown, and the rich, green land in the distance embodies the fertility and slow growth of the Queen. The Fool is the only Major Arcana card, so his energy dominates the spread. Wands are expansion, passion, and decisive action, as opposed to the stable, slow-moving Pentacles.

What's Your Story?

The Eight of Wands invites you to start getting out of your own way and let your magic fly to its target. Your careful preparations as the Queen of Pentacles are coming into alignment; you don't need to plan, budget, or ruminate further. And it's time to stop putting the needs of others first; nurture yourself and your intention so that it can fully manifest. Keep approaching your talisman magic with the optimism, faith, and trust of the Fool, knowing the universe is looking out for you.

Now that you have the basic information you need about talismans and tarot, let's move on to the process of creating and empowering your own talisman.

PART TWO

The Process

CHAPTER 6

Setting Your Intention

Now that you've laid the foundation for your magical work and gotten to know the tarot as your trusted advisor and companion, you're ready to focus on creating your talisman. Then we'll look at how you can use this magical tool to amplify your energy and increase your powers of manifestation. The first step is to set your intention—the purpose to which you will dedicate your talisman.

"Intention" is not a word I take lightly. It is a word that has weight and I use it with due consideration and respect. When you set an intention—not just in the context of this book—you tell yourself and the universe that you've identified what you need or want, and are committed to manifesting it. When speaking of talismans, I prefer using the word "intention" rather than the more common words "goal" or "target," because they seem to imply a duty, a task, or a competition in which you're forced to participate. You try to hit a goal; you might miss a target. The connotation of these words is that success is elusive and failure likely.

I'm also careful about using the words "wish" or "dream" in this context, because, on some level, they can denote something that is out of reach—miracles you wait for rather than desires on which you are empowered to act.

By contrast, an intention comes from your spirit and your force of will. Setting an intention is a deliberate magical act in which you choose the direction in which you want your life to go and act accordingly. An intention is like a tarot Ace—filled with potential. It encourages you to grab on to a brilliant idea and run with it, or to nurture your heart's desire so it can grow.

Before we start, take a couple of deep breaths and, as you exhale, release any expectations you may have and any tensions you may be feeling. Let them float away or sink into the earth. Even if you already have an idea of what you want to manifest with your talisman's support, allow yourself to be curious and open to possibilities—and above all, hopeful. Don't worry about locking in laser-sharp clarity around your intention; that will come later.

Ready?

CREATING POWERFUL INTENTIONS

There are three key aspects to creating powerful intentions: emotion, belief, and focus. When you harness your emotions in the service of your beliefs, and then focus that power on a positive change you want to manifest, that's when the magic happens.

Your intention is born from a need so strong that you are committed to working magic to fulfill it. As such, it should evoke a strong emotional response. How do you feel when you contemplate your intention? Are you excited? Hopeful? Inspired? Perhaps you're nervous, but committed to the path ahead. Imagine how you'll feel when you get that job, or establish an enriching and loving relationship, or move into the home that is just right for you. Imagine how empowered you will feel when you release old stories that are holding you back, or achieve whatever you need. Bring that emotion into your intention.

You don't need to know how you will do it, but you've got to *believe* that you can manifest your intention. When you send a message to the universe that you have faith in yourself, the universe answers and your desire begins to take on energetic momentum. Don't shy away from choosing a challenging or significant intention. But don't set your sights on something that you believe is impossible. Never invest your magical energies in something that you don't believe will bring results. Instead, let your intuition and emotions lead you to an intention that you believe, deep down, you will be able to manifest.

Always remember that magic's ultimate purpose is to foster positive change and spiritual growth for the person working it. And these benefits ripple out, making the world a better place as well. So when it comes to forming your intention, keep the focus firmly on yourself. Trying to change others or convince them to do what you desire is ethically unsound and tiptoes around the actual work. Use your emotions, your beliefs, and your focus to empower *your-self* through your intention. Real magic and lasting change come from within.

Types of Intentions

There are two types of intentions that are relevant to creating a talisman: quantifiable intentions and holistic intentions.

Quantifiable intentions work toward definite or measurable results—outcomes that are crystal clear when achieved. Timing is often an element in this type of intention. For example, you may form an intention to secure a new job before the end of the year, or manifest a certain amount of money within six months. Your intention may involve traveling to your dream destination for a milestone birthday, or completing a creative project by a deadline.

When working with this kind of magic, your best approach is to focus on manifesting the specific outcome while allowing events to unfold as needed. If you try to control precisely how your intention manifests, you may miss important opportunities or make the process more arduous than it needs to be. Trust in the universe and yourself, and work toward the desired outcome while releasing your hold on it.

If you are reading this book because you already have a quantifiable intention in mind, awesome! All I ask is that you keep an open mind as you go through this process. There are more layers to your intention waiting to be discovered, and the tarot will offer adjustments or expansion that can make your intention and its outcome more satisfying and transformational.

Holistic intentions are less measurable than quantifiable intentions, because they center around inner work like healing, spiritual development, or releasing narratives that no longer serve you well. They focus on well-being and quality of life rather than on fixed outcomes. They empower you to manifest ongoing and lasting change.

When you create a holistic intention, you celebrate milestones of growth along the way. Imagine you intend to increase your self-worth and self-confidence, or invite more joy into your life. Perhaps you want to foster forgiveness, or embrace your sovereignty. Rather than finally achieving a goal or being "finished," you create new patterns and ways of living and thriving.

Holistic intentions are compassionate and evolving. While it is still important to have a specific goal, holistic intentions allow you to shift that goal and change as you learn. They encourage you to experience challenges and grow through them. When you form a holistic intention, you release any attachment to an outcome and focus on building a sustainable practice that aligns with your values.

If you are leaning toward a holistic intention, that's wonderful! Your talisman will support you in this work now, and will be your faithful companion for as long as you wish. As with quantifiable intentions, I invite you to keep an open mind. The tarot will provide you with perspective and clarity around your desires and motivations. The cards will offer insights that make your intention more powerful, authentic, and nurturing.

MUSINGS

- At this point, do you have an idea whether your intention will be quantifiable or holistic?

- Which term resonates most with you: "goal," "target," "dream," "wish," or "intention"? Why?

EXPLORING YOUR INTENTION

Meditation and one-card tarot readings are both practices that can help you explore and evaluate your intention. As you ease into these practices, be open to discovering new or broader perspectives. Give your logical mind something else to do and tell your inner critic to go and take a nap. Let your intuition step forward to guide you.

Meditation

Meditation is a powerful tool for making magic and reading tarot. When you meditate, you learn how to focus your mind and understand your thoughts. Our minds often work overtime—worrying, daydreaming, planning for the future, or ruminating on the past. When you meditate, you pay attention to the present moment. You become sensitive to how you feel in your body, your frame of mind, and your emotional state. Meditation promotes calmness and clarity.

If you're new to meditation, don't worry; anyone can do it. Start by sitting comfortably or lying down, then focus on your breath. Feel your breath coming in and going out. Enjoy the constant, familiar rhythm. If thoughts come in, that's okay. Notice them, let them float away, and gently return to your breath. To begin, try meditating five or ten minutes a day and increasing the time when you're ready. Set a timer so you're not distracted by peeking at the clock.

Visualization can add another element to your meditation practice. When you use guided imagery to manifest a goal or achieve a state of being, you create a vivid scene in your mind and experience it as if it were happening right now. Visualization can increase your self-assurance, enhance your creativity, and strengthen your focus during meditation and beyond. When visualizing a desired outcome, you manifest it on an energetic level and attract it to you in the material world.

Meditation is a very personal experience, and your own practice will unfold as needed. Don't worry if you don't achieve immediate results. Sometimes you may go deep; sometimes you may fidget and wonder when it will be over. Just release any expectations you have and observe what you sense and feel. Over time and with consistent practice, you'll learn to enjoy the profound benefits meditation can bring.

The following meditation and visualization can help you check in with your body, mind, and spirit. It encourages you to explore where you are now, and understand what you need to thrive. When you do this magical work, you invite positive change into your life. When you take the time to go within and appreciate the value of this process, you can move forward with ease and clarity. Remember: You're doing this for *you*, and that's wonderful.

Meditation to Invite Positive Change

I recommend reading this meditation a few times before you start so you're familiar with its content and flow. This will make it easier for you to guide yourself through it. You can also record yourself reading it aloud and then play it back.

Find a quiet and restful place where you won't be disturbed. This time is just for you, so get cozy, light a candle, and turn off your phone. The rest of the world can wait for this brief time, and any tasks you have on your to-do list will still be there when you are done. Allow your thoughts to drift away, and tune into any sounds you hear around you. Perhaps you hear cars passing by, or birds singing, or rain falling, or a fan blowing.

Shift into a comfortable position. If you are sitting, place your feet flat on the floor and gently stretch your spine. If you prefer, you can lie down. When you are comfortably settled, soften your gaze or allow your eyes to close. Feel how your body connects with the surface you're seated or lying on. Feel the support that it offers you. At this moment, you are safe and held.

Inhale deeply and invite your body to relax as you exhale. Repeat this, then send your awareness around your body and notice where you are holding any tension. If you feel tension in your shoulders, neck, brow, or forehead, let it evaporate with each inhale and exhale. Let relaxation flow through your chest, your belly, and your legs, all the way down to your feet.

Imagine that a glowing white light surrounds your body, as if you're seated or lying within a luminous sphere. This sphere feels protective, but not restrictive. You know that it will grow and stretch with you while keeping you safe. Take a moment to enjoy this feeling. Let the light infuse your body, clearing any stagnant or negative energy.

Right now, you're taking the first steps toward creating your talisman. As you do, spend time with your most powerful and loving guides—your body, your mind, and your spirit. Ask these forces for guidance about the most beneficial intention you can set for your magical work.

Gently send your awareness to your belly. If it feels right to do so, rest your hand there. Feel it rise and fall with each breath. Let your belly relax and soften. What feeling do you get from this area of your body? Take a few moments to breathe and listen. Ask yourself: "What do I need to feel peace and ease here?" What is your gut, your intuition, trying to tell you? Do you hear a word or phrase? See an image? Get a feeling?

Now gently send your awareness to your heart. If it feels okay to do so, rest your hand there. Take a few moments to breathe and listen. Ask yourself:

"What does my heart need to feel nourished and full?" What is your heart, the core of your being, trying to tell you? Do you hear a word or a phrase? See an image? Get a feeling?

When you are ready, gently send your awareness to your brow, your Third Eye. If it feels right to do so, rest your fingers on the space between and above your eyebrows. Take a few moments to breathe and listen. Ask yourself: "What does my Third Eye want me to see?" What does your spirit, your higher self, need right now? Do you hear a word or phrase? See an image? Get a feeling?

Allow your awareness to flow through your body—first to your belly, then to your heart, then to your brow. Feel it flow through in a continuous loop. Relax, breathe, flow, and be open to any messages or feelings that you receive about the most beneficial and powerful intention you can set when creating your talisman.

Don't worry about getting specific right now. And know that you don't have to figure out how you will achieve this intention. Allow your inner voice to give you the first clues—the spark of inspiration, the starting point. Let your excitement build, knowing you're on the verge of change. Let the universe know you're ready. Breathe in and out slowly.

Give your imagination and your intuition freedom to play. What does your intention feel like? Do you feel a flutter in your belly or your heart? Is your Third Eye asking you to expand your perspective? Do you feel solid and grounded? Floating in the air? If you started this meditation with an intention in mind, how does it feel to you now? Were the messages you received in alignment with your preliminary intention? Did you go deeper? Or did a different kind of intention arise? Continue to breathe in and out slowly. Know that you've received the message that you need right now. It may not be clear at this point, but that's okay. Illumination will come.

Now you notice that the glowing, white light surrounding you is starting to fade away gently, until it finally disappears, leaving you with a blessing. You find yourself back in the place where you started this meditation. Before you return fully to your body, send some love and gratitude to yourself. You've taken a big step. You're doing this magical work to enrich your own life, to bring positive changes, and to put more light into the world. Your energy is shifting. Can you feel it?

When you're ready, take a deep breath in and release it. Shake out your hands and send any excess energy through the floor and into the earth. Move your head gently from side to side. Then open your eyes, feeling inspired and loved.

<><><><><><><><><><><><><><><><><><><><><><><><><><><><><><><><><><><><><><>

MUSINGS

- Write down anything you want to remember from this meditation. Let your thoughts flow; don't try to make them sensible or orderly.

- What does your belly need to feel peace and ease?

- What does your heart need to feel nourished and full?

- What does your Third Eye need you to see?

- What is the general theme of your intention? Were you surprised by it?

- Did you recognize your intention as quantifiable or holistic?

- Are there any other questions you want answered?

<><><><><><><><><><><><><><><><><><><><><><><><><><><><><><><><><><><><><><>

One-Card Tarot Reading

Once you've completed the meditation above, maintain your momentum by consulting your cards for more information. This one-card reading can help. As you shuffle your deck, reflect on the feelings and insights the meditation evoked for you. Then ask the tarot: "What intention is most beneficial for me right now?" Or: "What do I need to know about the magic I'll work with my talisman?"

When you're ready, pull one tarot card and place it face down in front of you. Take a deep breath and turn over the card. Allow yourself to experience an intuitive flash. Let your eyes roam over the card, and be open to any messages you receive. Notice how you felt when you first saw the image on the card. Did you laugh? Smile? Grimace? Did anything about the card jump out at you—symbols, colors, figures, creatures, numbers? Did a word or phrase pop into your mind?

Note what kind of card it is. Is it a Major Arcana card? If it's a Minor Arcana card, which suit is it? Is it a numbered card or a Court Card? This information will give you insight into the nature of your talisman intention. Remember: Major Arcana cards indicate life purpose, milestones, transitions, and spiritual paths. Wands denote creativity, career, ambition, and expansion. Cups suggest love, relationships, intuition, and connection. Swords relate to communication, conflict, peace of mind, and information. Pentacles represent well-being, finances, home, and job. The Court Cards are *you*—how you want to feel, the role you want to play, or the energy you need to embody to achieve your intention.

Take a good look at the scene on the card. Does it resemble a situation or experience that you desire? Or does it depict circumstances you're ready to bring to an end? Where are you in the scene? What are you doing? Follow your intuition. Try to relate the card to yourself—your situation, your needs, and your desires.

Finally, consider how the card relates to the insights you received in your meditation. Does it offer confirmation? Is it asking you to re-examine your perspective? Does it spark new questions, or introduce a different theme entirely?

When you've explored your intuitive and observational responses to the card, look back to the interpretations of the cards given in chapters 3 and 4. These will give you additional food for thought. Look particularly at the intention themes for each card and their keywords. These can spark ideas and suggest additional exploration if your card still leaves you puzzled.

If you're anxious or doubt your ability to interpret the card, you may be tempted to reach for the deck and pull one or more other cards, but don't do it. Resist the temptation to pull clarifying cards. Suck everything you can out of your one card. Take your time; luxuriate in it. If a mind-blowing, crystal-clear message doesn't immediately appear, that's okay. Trust that it will make itself known in its own good time. In chapter 10, you will find an in-depth tarot spread that may help answer your questions in more detail. For now, surrender to this one card.

Give yourself some space to contemplate your meditation experience and your one-card reading. Invite your dreams to send further insights. Place your card where you can see it for the next few days and be open to additional discoveries. You're in a place of possibilities, and magic is brewing. Let your imagination run away with you.

MUSINGS

- Which card did you draw? How did you feel when you first saw it?

- Did any symbol, figure, creature, color, or aspect of the card stand out for you?

- What did your card's title, suit, rank, or number mean to you?

- How does your card compare to your meditation experience?

- Did your card clarify or add to the theme of your intention? What is the theme of your intention now?

SAMPLE ONE-CARD SPREADS

Here are four examples of one-card spreads, including insights from the meditation above.

Nine of Pentacles

I did this reading for myself, asking what I needed to know about myself at that moment. My body, mind, and soul all sent me messages on a similar theme: *time*. My belly felt anxious from too many demands on my time. I'd been over-scheduling myself and underestimating my need for sleep. I was missing the company of loved ones and badly in need of relaxation. My heart told me I needed to have more faith in myself and that I didn't always have to prove myself worthy. My Third Eye wanted me to see that I am doing meaningful work and creating abundance, but I was wearing myself out along the way.

As I considered these thoughts, the general theme for my intention started to form: "I intend to continue to do the work I love with greater trust in my capabilities, less hustle, and more time to enjoy the life I'm creating."

When I pulled the Nine of Pentacles, I smiled and my body relaxed, because this card is one of my favorites. My eyes were drawn to the golden pentacle on which the woman rests her hand, and the ripe purple grapes behind her. The words "abundance" and "ease" came into my mind. On a personal note, I moved away from the big city out to wine country a few years ago, and this scene is an illustration of what I hoped to achieve by doing that. This felt like a beautiful affirmation of that choice.

The suit of Pentacles confirmed what came up in the meditation—a desire for rewarding work, financial abundance, less stress, and more time to enjoy life. I can get more specific about how I will approach that intention later, but this one-card spread gives me these clues: confidence, self-discipline, enjoyment, and independence.

The World

A client of mine did the same exercise with me, going into the meditation with retirement on her mind. She wondered if the time was right to focus on retirement and start a new, completely different, business venture.

Her body and belly felt peaceful and calm at the prospect of retirement, with no butterflies at all. Her heart was longing to say farewell to a career that was rewarding, but increasingly stressful and discouraging. Her Third Eye needed her to see new possibilities that had eluded her due to the demands of her job.

In her one-card reading, she pulled the World. She immediately saw herself as the central figure on the card and loved the freedom and power emanating from her. The wreath surrounding the floating figure then captured her

attention, suggesting victory and achievement. Because this was a Major Arcana card and the final card in the Fool's journey, she knew that her intention represented a significant milestone in her life.

We talked about the traditional meaning of the card—the triumphant culmination of a journey, life coming full circle, and a pause to appreciate what you've achieved before you transition into a new phase of life. All these meanings resonated with her desire to retire from her current career and start something new. The World showed her that her transition could be smooth if she left her job on a high note. She decided to consider what responsibilities she needed to fulfill or projects she had to complete before making her exit, so that she could move forward with pride in her accomplishments and without leaving behind any loose ends.

Ten of Swords

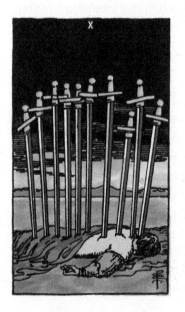

If you pull a challenging card or one that you don't like, you may be tempted to pop it back into the deck and choose another. Don't. Look for the helpful message it carries instead of dismissing it. Trust that the card came up for a reason. It may reveal a situation that needs to be addressed or shifted, or an aspect of yourself that needs compassion or release. Here's an example of what I'm talking about.

In the meditation, this client focused on her romantic relationship. She had been considering ending it for a long time, and wasn't sure why she was hesitating. Her belly told her that this relationship wasn't giving her what she needs—namely the assurance that she's loved and valued, and a priority in her partner's life. Her heart felt starved, needing affection and the joy of spending time with someone who delights in her company. Her Third Eye asked her to see that there is more for her, and that her partner's role in her life is complete. The general theme for her intention started to form—moving on from her current relationship and healing from its impact.

The card that came up for this reading was the Ten of Swords—a challenging and visceral image. My client's initial reaction was a sigh of resignation. She could feel the ache of the swords in her back, yet her focus was on the sunrise in the distance. The suit of Swords suggested a new way of thinking and an end to a lingering conflict. The card showed her that the first step in manifesting this change was accepting that a painful ending to her relationship could be a blessing in disguise. Her intention began here: "Let what needs to end end so I can heal and move forward lightly."

Queen of Pentacles

Another client decided to create a talisman to invite love into her life. She had been single for a long time and was unwilling to repeat old romantic patterns that kept letting her down, so she was open to possibilities. She hoped that the meditation and the cards would give her insight into the kind of love she needs right now—self-love, or romantic love, or both. She also mentioned that information about how to manifest that love would be extremely welcome.

QUEEN OF PENTACLES.

Her belly felt at ease and warm, and radiated confidence during the meditation. She knew she could trust the messages her intuition had been sending her, telling her that the time was right to focus on love. Her heart beat quickly but steadily, anticipating a new romance or connection. By nature, she is a romantic and hopeful person who often gets carried away by her emotions, so a good balance between her gut and her heart is essential. The message from her Third Eye was to look beyond the surface. Don't judge potential partners by appearance or weigh them against past loves or idealized ideas of what a soulmate should be. Go deeper. Her intention took shape as a desire to invite a romantic relationship into her life, a partnership that would be a source of happiness, passion, and support.

This client pulled the Queen of Pentacles. She was happy to see herself as a Queen, but dismayed that she was alone on the card. She was hoping for the Lovers or the Two of Cups. Still, this Queen told her that the first steps to a rewarding relationship are achieving contentment in your own company, confidence in your own capabilities, and independence in finances and home. She took the Queen's advice to heart.

In the next chapter, we will discuss how to choose the most powerful, personal, and meaningful material for your talisman, based on what you have discovered about your intention.

CHAPTER 7

Choosing Your Talisman

Now that you have discovered the overall theme of your intention, it's time to choose the material you'll use for your talisman.

Your talisman is the physical embodiment of your magic. It is intimately connected with your intention, and holds and amplifies your energy and force of will. So the material you choose to make it must be wise, powerful, and personal. As you read through this chapter and consider your options, keep two ideas in mind. Select a material that aligns with the nature of your intention. And choose an object you will love wearing or carrying—one that gives you pleasure when you look at it.

Creating a talisman is an act of sympathetic magic. Its power is based in the belief that like attracts like, that like produces like, and that effects resemble their cause. So your talisman needs to be made of a material that shares an affinity, a characteristic, or a connection with your desired result in order to manifest your intention. For instance, a heart-shaped charm or a rose-quartz pendant can invite romance or foster greater self-compassion, because these materials are associated with love.

The word "sympathy" implies sharing emotion and connection. If you are sympathetic toward someone, you think that you understand what that person is experiencing. Being sympathetic can also imply wanting to help in the midst of a challenge. You may feel compassion for someone and want to help that person if you can. A talisman's magic is based on this same idea of connection and shared feelings or experiences. When you perform magic to consecrate a talisman and imbue it with your intention, it becomes an extension of you. You are positively affected by its properties and powers, and you work together as a powerful team to manifest your desire.

LOVING YOUR TALISMAN

In addition to choosing a material based on its spiritual and energetic properties, it's important that you select an object that you love, and that fascinates you. You will be working with this object and keeping it close to you until you manifest your intention, so it should make you happy to look at it and touch it. It should be comfortable to wear and feel good on your skin. When you fall in love with your talisman and become best friends with it, this emotional connection will bolster its power and effectiveness.

For instance, I adore wearing jewelry and often work with it when creating my talismans. Pendants are my favorite because, when you wear one, you feel it on your skin close to your heart. You warm it with your body's heat. You can keep it hidden, or you can display it proudly.

Rings also make powerful talismans. You can easily see them as you go about your day, and you are aware of them every time you type on a keyboard, or pick up your phone, or gesture during a conversation. In fact, you connect with them when doing any of the many tasks you perform with your hands. Traditionally, rings bind you to a promise and are associated with unity and eternity.

Pendants, rings, bracelets, anklets, pins, and earrings all make wonderful talismans. Just choose the piece you are happiest wearing. When you wear it, feel the weight of it and let that remind you of the intention it represents. When you put it on, make it a ritual that reaffirms the magic you performed when you transformed it into a talisman. Let it become a renewal of your commitment to your intention and your collaboration with the universe.

Ideally, a talisman should always be close to you when you're in manifestation mode, rather than placed on your altar or tucked away in a drawer. If you don't like wearing jewelry, choose an object small enough to fit in your pocket so you can carry it with you easily. Remain aware of its energy and presence just as you would with a piece of jewelry, and stay open to any signs and synchronicities it draws to you throughout your day.

There are many materials to choose from as you consider creating your talisman. In fact, you can use just one primary material, or you can combine several to weave in extra magical details. For instance, you can choose a crystal as your primary material and then add a silver bail or setting, calling on the properties of both. Or you can choose a gold charm in the shape of a symbol or a mythical creature, or use a treasured heirloom that contains a gemstone or has symbolic significance. You don't need to over-complicate things; simple is good. Just be aware of possibilities and materials that complement each other.

There are several categories of materials you can consider as you decide how to fashion your talisman. I give you some examples below, although this is by no means a comprehensive list. In fact, your talisman can be made of any material that is meaningful to you and will connect with your intention. Let your imagination play, and get creative. That's how you make magic.

<><><><><><><><><><><><><><><><><><><><><><><><><><><><><><><><><><><><><><><><>

MUSINGS

- Do you wear jewelry? If so, what kind?

- Consider a piece of jewelry that you love and ask yourself why it is special to you.

- Would you consider using a piece of jewelry for your talisman?

<><><><><><><><><><><><><><><><><><><><><><><><><><><><><><><><><><><><><><><><>

CRYSTALS

My lifelong love of crystals, minerals, and stones started with a school field trip to a local science center when I was eight or nine. Everyone was excited to see a giant metal ball that crackled with static electricity. If you were lucky, you got to put your hand on it and see your hair fly up and stick out straight around you, amazing your classmates and giving you momentary celebrity status. They didn't pick me for that honor, but thanks to my mom, who was a volunteer chaperone that day, I did leave the gift shop with a precious treasure—two small pyrite cubes in a white box with a see-through plastic lid. The pyrite felt heavy and solid in my hand, and I loved its nickname—fool's gold. Those rocks were clearly getting away with something, and it felt as if we were sharing a joke. I carried that little box everywhere, peering at the minerals through the lid, careful not to drop or lose them.

Now ambling around a crystal shop is one of my favorite pastimes. Sometimes I have a stone in mind—rose quartz for self-love, obsidian for protection and grounding, amethyst for divination. But the magic happens when a crystal calls out to me and I can't ignore it or leave it behind. Then I know that's the one I need.

Crystals are hands-down my favorite material for creating talismans, because they have beneficial qualities and spiritual superpowers that are inherent in their structure. When you bring your vibration into resonance with theirs, you take on these qualities. For example, sparkly purple lepidolite calms the heart and mind, and releases stress and worry. When you work with it, you enjoy these benefits. If you want to attract financial abundance into your life, green aventurine will share its luck and confidence with you.

Moreover, crystals are natural recording devices. You can program them with your intention and desire using ritual, visualization, and meditation. You can pour your energy into them, and they hold it and radiate it outward, supporting you and drawing what you need to you. In addition to holding your initial intention, crystals record the information and knowledge you gather as you manifest your goal. When you wear or carry them, they enhance your energy and add power to your intention. For example, if you want to amplify your creativity and passion, choose a stone like fire agate that has those characteristics. If clear and open communication is your objective, blue lace agate can boost your skills.

Crystals, gemstones, and minerals are all natural marvels. Their beautiful and elegant complexity reminds us of how magnificent our world is. They come from the earth and are manifestations of its energy, just as we are. Because we're made of the same basic materials, we can feel that connection. Crystals help us access the wisdom of the earth and communicate with the universe.

The shape of a crystal can also add a layer of power to your magic. Points act like magic wands to radiate outward energy. Spheres gently surround you with protective and embracing forces. Double-pointed crystals enhance two-way communication with the Divine and your higher self, sending and receiving messages. Cubes have a solid, secure, and grounding energy. The solid bases of pyramids support you as you expand and stretch upward toward the apex.

Carved crystals also have special meanings. Teardrops suggest healing from sadness; hearts invite love and compassion. Squares are stable and orderly, while ovals or egg shapes represent fertility, life, and rebirth. Crystals shaped like flora or fauna express the characteristics of the creature or plant represented. Raw or unpolished stones have an intense and wild energy, and facilitate a deep connection. By contrast, polished or faceted stones reveal beauty that might otherwise be hidden; they also can be more comfortable to wear against your skin.

The crystals below are some of my favorites. They have brought me excellent results, and I hope you use them to spark further exploration. I've organized the list by general themes or intentions, and I've limited the number of examples for each to three. So this is certainly not an exhaustive list. I recommend that you read through the whole list before choosing a category (or more than one) that resonates with your intention. Then see if any of the crystals listed there stand out to you.

Once you have a short list of crystals you'd like to get to know better, visit your local crystal shop or search out images in books or online. Use the knowledge you gain from this chapter, combined with your intuition, to choose the crystal that feels right to you. If the stone that attracts you most doesn't precisely align with your intention, don't reject it. Consider its properties and ask yourself if it offers a beneficial quality that you can weave into your magic.

Abundance and Prosperity

Green and gold stones tend to resonate with all forms of abundance—financial gain, lavish lifestyle, releasing a scarcity mindset, general well-being and thriving, and an awareness of blessings, joy, and opportunities. Achieving a state of abundance comes down to confidence, force of will, and optimism, with a little luck and daring thrown in.

- *Citrine:* a golden crystal that radiates solar energy, inspiring optimism and confidence while attracting wealth and supporting the manifestation of desires. Its creative power fires up your imagination and a belief that anything is possible.

- *Green aventurine:* an opaque stone the color of a green apple, with sparkly inclusions. It fosters prosperity, growth, and good luck. As a heart-centered stone, it encourages you to pursue joy and welcome positive change.

- *Honey calcite:* a honey-colored transparent or translucent stone that looks like candy and emanates sweet and luscious energy. It assists you in manifesting abundance with confidence, and melts away a scarcity mindset or a sense of being overwhelmed.

Clarity and Direction

This category includes mainly colorless stones. Clarity refers to a clear vision of the future, supportive and accurate thinking, and gaining the understanding or information you need to make good decisions and move forward.

- *Apophyllite:* a clear stone that often forms in pyramidal clusters that sparkle like ice. It enhances meditation, divination, psychic awareness, and communication with spirit guides. It shines a light on difficult situations.

- *Clear quartz:* a colorless stone commonly formed in hexagonal prisms with points at one or both ends. This is the ultimate all-purpose crystal, a must-have in your toolbox. It clears negative or stagnant energy and keeps you flowing so that your perception is sharp and communication channels are open. Combine it with other crystals to amplify their qualities.

- *Selenite:* a transparent or translucent stone with some striations that form in flat plates that look like window glass. If it is fibrous and white, it is most likely satin spar, a related mineral that is much more common and relatively inexpensive. Selenite clears your aura, dissolves energy blockages, and facilitates communication with spirit guides and your higher self. It has a calming and peaceful energy. Named after the

Greek goddess of the moon, Selene, it shares a connection with that luminous celestial body.

Communication

These crystals are generally blue. They facilitate open communication, speaking authentic truth, being heard, and active listening. They support those who work in professions that rely on communication skills, like writing, public speaking, and marketing.

- *Amazonite:* a green-blue semi-opaque stone, like a robin's egg. It gives you the courage to speak your truth and the skill to communicate effectively. Speaking your intentions aloud is the first step toward realizing them, making this stone powerful for manifestation magic.

- *Aquamarine:* a clear, pale-blue stone, like a tropical sea. It is calming and refreshing, and cools heated arguments. It guides you through your emotional depths and supports you in expressing your feelings. This stone is beloved by mermaids.

- *Blue lace agate:* a stone that is banded in circular patterns of light-blue and white. It counteracts self-doubt and adds conviction and power to your words. It is a gentle stone of quiet words and effective communication that facilitates articulate, authentic speech, as opposed to saying too much or rambling.

Confidence

This category contains mainly red, yellow, and orange stones. Confidence relates to courage, ambition, and trust in yourself and your capabilities. It inspires you to go outside of your comfort zone, expand your vision, and dare to go after something big.

- *Carnelian:* a deep red-orange stone that bolsters courage and combats fears. It inspires leadership, self-esteem, and taking bold action toward your goals. It is an energizing stone, excellent for combatting procrastination.

- *Mahogany obsidian:* a stone that is a mixture of black, red, and reddish-brown in spotted and swirling patterns. Its grounding energy supports you in healing imposter syndrome, releasing shame, and reclaiming your power.

- *Pyrite:* gold crystals with a metallic luster that form in cubes and octahedrons. Also known as fool's gold, it shields you from negative energy and criticism. It attracts abundance and wealth, and inspires you to go after what you want with vigor.

Creativity

These are mainly red, orange, and gold stones. Creativity can relate to a specific project you're working on, expressing your passion and vision, or metaphorically birthing something new.

- *Fire agate:* orange, brown, red, green, and gold stones that look like a bright flame. This stone feeds your inner fire, moves you through creative blockages, and gives you the courage to express yourself passionately. It reminds you that you're a human being of flesh and blood, and gives you an appreciation of the physical world that offers much pleasure and wisdom.

- *Garnet:* a glassy, deep-red stone that resembles a pomegranate seed. It helps you overcome resistance, express creativity, and bring ideas to fruition. This is a stone of simmering passion, self-confidence, and devotion.

- *Tangerine quartz:* an orange stone whose color comes from iron-oxide inclusions that form in clusters and points. It has a joyful energy filled with curiosity, playfulness, and a willingness to learn. It invites you to embrace new possibilities and find purpose in your passions.

Healing

Crystals provide many kinds of healing, including healing emotional wounds and trauma, grief, familial or ancestral patterns, forgiveness for yourself or others, letting go of what no longer serves, and starting a practice of self-care and well-being.

- *Green tourmaline:* a light-green stone that suggests spring growth and tender shoots. Its striated crystals may be long rods or triangular, often held in a quartz matrix. It channels nature's healing power and releases the emotional burdens you've been carrying. It has a calming and soothing energy.

- *Rhodochrosite:* a light-pink to red stone with zigzag-patterned white bands, the color of a rose. This stone's superpower is unconditional self-love and self-acceptance, which leads to peace and healing. It is tender and gentle, and invites your inner child to come out and play.

- *Ruby fuchsite:* a naturally occurring composite of red ruby and green fuchsite. This stone blends the calming and nurturing energy of fuchsite with the vitality and courage of ruby, producing harmony and well-being. It promotes healing by encouraging you to love and value your true self.

Intuition and Psychic Work

These are primarily white, purple, and violet stones. This category refers to actual divination practice, increasing psychic abilities, or having greater trust in your intuition and inner voice. It involves opening your Third Eye and seeing the unseen.

- *Amethyst:* a gorgeous rich, dark purple. This stone uplifts your spirit while bringing you to a place of calm and peace. It facilitates deep meditation and reaching higher states of consciousness. It protects during psychic or spiritual practices without blocking your awareness.

- *Labradorite:* a vivid rainbow stone with flashes of color—blue, gold, green, orange, violet. This stone shimmers like the Northern Lights. It is a magical stone for diviners, spiritual seekers, and healers, enhancing intuition and psychic abilities. It calms the mind and helps you use your voice and speak with confidence. In spiritual or divination work, it is a protective stone that connects you with your magical powers.

- *Moonstone:* a white stone with a sheen and brilliant flashes of blue. It supports and stimulates intuition, psychic gifts, and a connection with the magic of the moon and the Goddess. It balances your energy and helps you flow with the cycles of life. It supports dream work, spiritual exploration, and growth. It is the energy of the Full Moon in her glory.

Love

This category includes mainly pink and green stones. It covers all kinds of love—inviting love into your life, seeking romance or a soulmate/partner, healing or improving relationships, self-love and self-compassion, and friendship.

- *Kunzite:* a light-pink or mauve stone formed of prismatic crystals with striations. It is a stone of harmony, facilitating communication between your heart and mind, and give-and-take between you and the people you love. It encourages you to receive love without question and to offer it unconditionally. This gentle stone also eases heartbreak.

- *Malachite:* an opaque stone with swirls of light and deep, dark green. This is a heart-healing stone that protects you from negative energy and infuses your aura with positivity and luck. It clears emotional blockages and balances mood swings.

- *Rose quartz:* a translucent, soft-pink stone that embodies love. It opens your heart and infuses you with universal love energy that you, in turn, radiate out to the world. It assures you that you are worthy of love, you are loved, and you have love to offer the world. Invite love into all aspects of your life with this calming and heart-healing crystal.

Protection and Grounding

These are mainly dark and heavy stones. They protect against external negative energy and help you feel grounded, present, and connected to your body.

- *Barite:* a dense, heavy tabular-shaped stone that is often white or colorless, but sometimes yellow, red, or brown. It keeps you grounded and anchored in your body during spiritual practice, meditation, astral travel, or dream work. It has a calming and practical energy.

- *Black obsidian:* a glossy black volcanic glass that acts as a shield against negative energy and attachments. It is a powerful support for spiritual work, connecting you with the solid earth beneath you and easing stress and nervous tension. Because of its glassy sheen, it is often used as a scrying mirror.

- *Black tourmaline:* striated crystals that may be long rods or triangular. This is a must-have psychic shield, as it absorbs negative energies and repels unwanted entities during ritual work and everyday life. It is believed to protect against radiation and electromagnetic fields commonly emitted by cell phones, computers, and other electronic devices.

Peace of Mind

These stones are generally purple and blue. They release anxiety and worry, calm the mind, and foster trust in yourself and the universe.

- *Celestite:* delicate, pale, translucent blue stone that gently uplifts and activates your inner vision, and opens communication with angelic beings and spirit guides. Its energy is diffuse rather than focused; it will purify a room and fill it with serenity.

- *Fluorite:* a gentle but powerful stone that contains swirls of green and purple in varying intensities. The green supports emotional healing and self-love, while the purple boosts intuition, connection with spirit, and raising vibrations. It is perfect for spiritual spring cleaning, as it helps you clear out negativity and scattered energies.

- *Lepidolite:* a lilac or deep-purple stone with mica sparkles. This lithium-rich crystal can release stress and worry, soothe emotional extremes, and promote peaceful sleep. It is a supportive companion during times of transition and significant life changes.

Success and Victory

These stones support career, legal situations, personal goals, competitions, or contests. They boost confidence, as victory often comes down to having the self-assurance to act toward your desired outcome.

- *Bloodstone:* an opaque, dark-green stone with red spots. It protects from danger, conflict, and hostility, and helps overcome enemies and challenges to sovereignty without fear. It will increase your chances of success in a dispute or legal matter.

- *Sunstone:* an orange and reddish-brown stone with glittering inclusions. It is the epitome of solar energy—leadership, ambition, manifestation of your desires, and sharing your gifts generously. It lifts your mood, boosts your self-worth, and bathes you in optimism.

- *Tiger eye:* a stone with yellow, gold, and brown bands and a luminous luster. It motivates you to take bold and strategic action, while giving you the energy and stamina to see things through. It helps you face challenges with calm, courage, and keen senses.

Shadow Work

These often black or dark stones shimmer with flecks of light that support revealing, acknowledging, and integrating your shadow self in order to foster healing, unity, and self-acceptance.

- *Nuummite:* an ancient black stone with flashes and flecks of iridescent gold found only in a remote area of Greenland. Combining darkness and light, it gives you the courage to go into the shadows, release what no longer serves, and return to the light. It is protective and grounding, enhancing psychic abilities, shamanic journeying, and manifestation magic.

- *Smoky quartz:* a pale-brown to deep-black transparent-to-opaque stone whose grounding energy guides you through fear, stress, and dark nights of the soul. It purifies negative energy and ends unhelpful behavior patterns and beliefs.

- *Snowflake obsidian:* a black stone with white or gray spots that resemble snowflakes. It inspires hope during challenging times by focusing on the bright side and offering new ideas and solutions. This crystal of light and darkness facilitates past-life recall and communication with loved ones who have passed on.

Spiritual Path and Life Purpose

These stones are of all colors. They help you understand your calling, your purpose, or your path to higher spiritual development, and show you how to follow it.

- *Astrophyllite:* a bronze, brown, and golden-yellow stone that forms in blades or rays that radiate out like a star. It sends light into your shadow self so that you can achieve self-acceptance, healing, and wholeness. It helps you understand how to live in alignment with your purpose and divine plan.

- *Charoite:* a light- to deep-purple stone with inclusions of black, white, and gold. It reveals your true, sacred path and guides you toward your highest, most joyful purpose. It helps you recognize signs and synchronicities, and act upon them effectively, while keeping you grounded and protected.

- *Seraphinite:* a deep, forest-green stone that is named for the seraphim, the highest order of angels, because its silvery markings resemble the feathers of angel wings. It helps you communicate with angels, guardians, and higher spiritual realms. A stone of grace and spiritual growth, it provides healing energy to the body, mind, and spirit.

MUSINGS

• Do you find any of the crystals on the list intriguing? If so, why? And which ones?

• Did you find a crystal that matches your intention?

• Will you work with a crystal for your talisman?

∞∞∞

METALS

Like crystals, metals have their own characteristics and qualities. The two categories of metals to consider when crafting your talisman are precious metals and base metals.

Precious metals include gold, platinum, and silver. Gold resonates with solar energy, God, spiritual perfection, success, and protection. Platinum supports stability, strength, endurance, and nobility. Silver connects with lunar energy, the Goddess, intuition, instinct, and divination.

Base metals include brass, bronze, and copper. Brass, which is an alloy of copper and zinc, denotes healing, courage, protection, and prosperity. Bronze, which is an alloy of copper and tin, supports emotional balance, vitality, resilience, and success. Copper, which is an unalloyed metal, represents healing, conducting energy, electricity, and communication.

As with all the materials listed in this chapter, you can work with one primary metal or add layers of meaning by combining them. For instance, if you intend to support your divination practice and increase your psychic awareness, you can choose a labradorite pendant set in sterling silver, as both materials have that property. Or you can choose a lion-shaped brass ring to foster courage, or a copper-wrapped amazonite pendant to help you communicate with strength and clarity.

When it comes to metals, I gravitate toward silver for its connection to the moon and the Goddess. The cool, lunar energy resonates with me as a diviner, as an introvert, and as an empath. Although metals aren't usually my primary talisman material, I often layer silver onto a crystal or find a version of a symbol in silver, which makes the talisman feel very personal and reflective of who I am.

I don't recommend using silver-plated or gold-plated talismans, however, because they aren't durable. The base metal interior and its properties are revealed when the plating wears off.

◇◇

MUSINGS

- Do you gravitate toward any particular metal? If so, why?

- Do you have any sensitivities or allergies to metals?

◇◇

SYMBOLIC REPRESENTATIONS

Rather than focusing on the material itself, you can also take a figurative approach to your talisman and choose an object in the form of a symbol that fits your intention. For example, you can work with a coin or a piece of jewelry shaped like a dollar sign to attract money and prosperity. The material adds another layer of meaning, of course. For instance, a gold dollar sign reinforces your desire to manifest wealth, and a four-leaf clover carved from green aventurine is extra lucky.

Here is a partial list of symbolic representations that may spark your imagination.

- *Achievement and success:* crown, sun, star, wreath, arrow

- *Ancestors:* human figure, skull, tree, family crest

- *Career:* something specific to your profession or the job you desire

- *Source energy and the Divine:* angel, solar cross, Merkaba, Metatron's Cube

- *Creativity:* pen, musical note or treble clef, paintbrush, book, musical instrument, or something specific to your creative intention

- *Intuition and psychic ability:* eye, pomegranate, moon

- *Love:* heart, rose, ring, knot

- *Money:* coin, dollar sign, rainbow and pot of gold, fish, representation of what you would use the money to buy or achieve

- *Opening the way or revealing knowledge or information:* key, open book, door

- *Protection:* angel, pentacle, Evil Eye, hand

- *Travel:* wings, globe, train, bus, car, boat

- *Well-being and longevity:* ankh, flower of life, apple, infinity sign

MUSINGS

- Do you already have a connection with any symbols? Do they relate to your intention?

- Tarot cards are rich with symbolism. Revisit the card you pulled for your one-card reading in chapter 6. Are there any symbols on it that suggest a talisman to you?

FOUND OBJECTS

You can also let your material find you by communicating your intention to the universe and keeping your eyes open for what appears. Even if you have an idea of the kind of object you're watching for, allow yourself to be surprised.

Nonetheless, even if you invite your object to find you, you still have to go about the process purposefully. Go for a walk in nature or stroll through the city with your intention foremost in your heart and mind. Let your intuition guide you. Be observant and watch for the right object to appear. Sometimes found objects appear from nature—like feathers, acorns, chestnuts, unusual stones, cat's whiskers, or four-leaf clovers. A coin, a key, or a shiny object may catch your eye. Or someone may give you an unexpected gift. Regardless of how or when the object appears, it will inform you further about your intention, so pay close attention. If it's a feather, what kind of bird did it come from? If it's a coin, what year was it minted? What currency is it? What denomination?

Once, on a talisman-hunting nature walk along a forest trail near my home, I came upon an angel ornament hanging in a tree. The angel was playing a trumpet and it reminded me of the Judgement card. I almost claimed it as my talisman, but I decided to give thanks for the message of guidance and encouragement, and leave it in place for other wanderers to discover.

◇◇

MUSINGS

- What's the most fascinating or meaningful object you've found unexpectedly?

- Would you like to work with a found object, or would you prefer to choose your material?

◇◇

OBJECTS WITH PERSONAL SIGNIFICANCE

You may already have something in your possession that perfectly fits your intention—perhaps an heirloom, or something with family or ancestral ties, or a gift from a loved one, or a childhood treasure. Objects like these call on memories, love, or ancestral support, so they are especially effective for intentions that focus on healing family patterns or connecting with your heritage.

In this case, while its significance to you remains its most critical aspect, consider what the object is made of and its shape. My dear aunt used a stamp for a wax seal of our family crest to create silver pendants for us. When I wear mine, I feel the love that went into making it and the support of my family line. My intention is to embody my ancestors' resilience and love of life, and appreciate the extraordinary, loving family that I'm part of right now.

〰〰〰〰〰〰〰〰〰〰〰〰〰〰〰〰〰〰〰〰〰〰〰〰〰〰〰〰

MUSINGS

- Do you have an object in your possession that fits your intention well?

- A piece with personal significance is charged with memory and emotion. Are you considering working with an object like this for your talisman? Or would you prefer to work with an object that is new and clear of associations?

〰〰〰〰〰〰〰〰〰〰〰〰〰〰〰〰〰〰〰〰〰〰〰〰〰〰〰〰

Animals and Mythical Creatures

You can also craft your talisman in the form of an animal or mythical creature with characteristics you admire and intend to embody. Pendants, metal jewelry, figurines, toys, carved crystals—or anything meaningful to you, for that matter—can come to resonate with the qualities of any animal or creature you choose. I wear a small, silver fox-shaped earring to remind me to be clever and mischievous, and a ring with a silver bee and a peridot to keep me productive and focused.

Here are just a few ideas to get you thinking about how you can use the shapes of animals and mythical creatures to support your intention.

- *Bear:* strength, protection, healing

- *Cat:* independence, curiosity, witchcraft and magic

- *Deer:* gentleness, calm, agility

- *Dog:* loyalty, companionship, vigilance

- *Dolphin:* harmony, joy, communication

- *Dove:* peace, love, hope

- *Dragon:* wealth, longevity, strength

- *Eagle:* victory, freedom, courage

- *Fish:* wealth, fertility, abundance

- *Fox:* cleverness, trickery, taking risks that pay off

- *Lion:* nobility, courage, strength

- *Mermaid:* transformation, beauty, sensuality

- *Owl:* wisdom, ancestral work, foresight and insight

- *Phoenix:* rebirth, new start, reinvention

- *Rabbit:* fertility, speed, resilience

- *Raven:* prophecy, intelligence, trickster

- *Selkie:* shapeshifting, adaptability, resilience

- *Snake:* rebirth, transformation, healing

- *Sphinx:* wisdom, mystery, protection

- *Unicorn:* purity, grace, miracles

- *Wolf:* instinct, loyalty, communication

If you have an affection for any animal or mythical creature, ask yourself why. Then consider whether you can imagine an animal or mythical creature with characteristics that match your intention.

Now that you've explored all these categories, you are ready to choose your material. In the next chapter, we will discuss how to clear and prepare your talisman so that it's ready to receive your intention.

CHAPTER 8

Preparing Your Talisman

Before we start considering how to prepare your talisman for your magical work, let's take a moment to reflect on how far you've come. You've already invested a lot of time and effort into formulating your intention and finding the talisman that best embodies it. It may not have been easy to decide on just one object; it may have been a challenge to find just what you were looking for. But you accepted that challenge and devoted a lot of introspection, self-knowledge, curiosity, and courage to making the right choice. So take a moment to congratulate yourself on having taken these significant steps forward. You've committed yourself to manifesting an intention that will bring positive change into your life, and that's exciting. Now it's time to connect with the emotion that your intention sparks and anticipate great results. Before you can do that, however, you have to empower your talisman to support your magic.

There are several different ways to prepare a talisman, but perhaps the most important is called "clearing." When you clear an object, you remove any energies it may retain from previous use or contact. You don't clear or remove any characteristics of the material or its qualities. You just remove any impressions it may have picked up during its journey to get to you. If an object was made by someone else, or owned by someone before you, or purchased in a shop or online, it's likely gone through many hands and absorbed a lot of energies along the way. Even if the object comes from your personal belongings, you may have worn it or used it for another purpose, and it may have absorbed your own energy and intentions. But no matter where your talisman came from or who used it before you, you can return it to its natural state by clearing it, thereby making it a blank slate that you can imbue with your intention so it can support your manifestation magic.

There are two types of clearing used in magical work—preparing objects when you start working with them, and regularly clearing objects with which you have worked. Indeed, the practice of clearing is not just for talismans. It is good practice to clear your tarot cards and any magical tools you use on a regular basis. In fact, it's good practice to clear yourself as well to remove negative energies you may have attracted. In this chapter, we'll consider methods for an initial, all-out clearing of a talisman to prepare it for use. This practice is not negative or punitive in any way. It's simply a way to show your talisman love and care, and deepen your bond with it.

One caveat. It is important to consider the material your talisman is made of so you can avoid clearing methods that may damage it. Water, salt, earth, or a damp night in the moonlight won't agree with flakey or brittle crystals, or paper, or other fragile and porous objects.

CLEARING OBJECTS

There are many ways to clear an object and, as with everything in our magical world, I encourage you to choose the method that makes the most sense to you. I recommend that you try several of the techniques below to find the one that works best for you. But no matter which method you choose, take your time. Enjoy it. Sink into it. Even something as simple as clearing your talisman can be a ritual and a thread in the magic you are weaving.

In most of the descriptions below, I don't specify how long it takes to do an effective clearing, because I don't think there is a prescribed amount of time required for any of these methods to work. Use your intuition, and work within your limitations of time, space, and materials. Your intention to clear is the most critical factor here. The tools I suggest are merely helpers and amplifiers.

Once you have cleared your talisman, however, there are ways you can check to determine if you were successful. For instance, you can hold a pendulum above it and ask: "Is my talisman cleared?" Give your pendulum time to swing. Your work is done if it swings in the pattern that indicates "yes" for you. If it swings in a pattern that you recognize as "no," repeat the clearing or try a different method. You can also ask your pendulum to guide you to the best clearing method and the length of time it requires. Be sure to ask only "yes" or "no" questions.

You can also use your intuition to tell you if your talisman is successfully cleared. Center yourself by sitting quietly and breathing in a slow deep pattern. Hold your talisman cupped in your hands and notice what you feel. Try to tune in to its energy. Do you sense lightness and clarity, or heaviness that still needs clearing? Trust your gut and act accordingly.

Common methods for clearing talismans and other magical tools include burning incense, visualization, sound, water, moonlight, and burial. Let's take a look at each one in more detail.

Incense

When you burn incense, the fragrant smoke clears both the object and the surrounding environment. Since incense permeates the space, choose a scent that you enjoy—one that is calming and uplifting, or that reminds you of sacred places. Some traditional types of incense used for clearing are lavender, rosemary, bay, pine, cedar, copal, or frankincense. These commonly come in cones or sticks that burn easily when lit, but you can also burn herbs or resins by placing them on burning coals.

When you're ready to clear your talisman, gather together the incense you want to use, a fire-proof container or holder, and matches or a lighter. Carefully light the incense, then hold your talisman in your hand and waft it slowly through the smoke clockwise. Envelop it in the smoke and fragrance for as long as you feel necessary. This method of clearing can be a lovely meditative activity that gives you a chance to look at your talisman from all angles, appreciate its beauty, and bond with it.

Be mindful when burning anything or using a flame of any kind not to let your attention wander too much. And always be sure that the incense is fully extinguished when you're done.

Visualization

When you use visualization to clear your talisman, you call on your intention and your magical energy. You can do this anywhere at any time, and you don't need any special tools—just yourself.

Before you begin, find a comfortable space where you won't be disturbed. Center and ground yourself with a few deep breaths. When ready, hold your talisman in your non-dominant hand and let your other hand hover above it. Close your eyes and visualize a bright, white light flowing from your hands. Invite that light to permeate your talisman, while stating your intention to clear any stagnant or negative energy in preparation for your magical work.

Settle your breath into a slow gentle pattern and connect with your talisman. Continue to visualize white light clearing it. Imagine that you can see the unwanted energy drifting out and away. When you feel as if your talisman is cleared, release your connection to it and offer gratitude to spirit, your higher self, and the earth for supporting you in this work.

Sound

Sound is an effective way to clear objects without the fire, smoke, and fragrance of incense. Moreover, sound won't damage delicate items the way water, earth, or salt can.

All objects have a natural frequency at which they vibrate. And we know that sound, which is energy created by vibrations, has a profound effect on us. Music can uplift our spirits and calm our minds. Fire alarms or construction noise can jangle our nerves. When you create a high-vibration or pleasing sound in the vicinity of your talisman, those sound waves clear unwanted or low-vibration energies from it.

There are various ways you can work with sound. Chiming a singing bowl or ringing a bell over and around your talisman will clear it—with the added benefit that you'll also enjoy the calming effects. You can also use your voice to sing or chant over your talisman. Beating a drum, shaking a rattle, or clapping your hands can also create vibrations that clear and energize.

Water

This method is as simple as placing your talisman under running water. Of course, putting it in a beautiful lake or river or ocean is ideal. But kitchen or bathroom tap water works just as well. As you hold or place your talisman under the water, envision it being cleansed and cleared. Again, don't use water for more delicate materials or flakey or brittle stones, because you may damage them.

Moonlight

I like to clear my crystals or other magical objects in the light of a Full Moon. You can do this during any phase of the moon, but the Full Moon packs the most power. Put your talisman on a windowsill or a table near a window for a moon bath, or put it outside somewhere safe. As with cleansing by water, be careful if your talisman is delicate and might be affected by rain or dew. I put mine in position when the moon rises and leave it there overnight. This also allows you to commune with the moon, perhaps asking that you be sent some dreams about your talisman and your magical intention while bathed in that lovely light. And don't worry if it's a cloudy night or you don't have a clear view of the moon. The energy will still be there.

Burial

Burying an object in salt, earth, or rice is an effective way to draw out unwanted energies. If you use a container filled with salt or rice, throw it away after you've completed your clearing. When burying your talisman in the earth, find a safe spot that you will be able to locate later—perhaps in your yard or in a potted plant. Wrap delicate objects in fabric or paper before you bury them. How long you leave them buried is up to you. I usually leave my objects buried for at least twenty-four hours.

MUSINGS

- Choose a method to clear your talisman. Why did you choose that method?

- How did it work for you?

BONDING WITH YOUR TALISMAN

Once you have cleared your talisman, spend some time getting to know it. The meditation below can help you forge a bond between you and your talisman, and attune to each other's energy. This will give you a sense of what it will be like to work your magic together. During the meditation, introduce yourself and be open to discovering a friend, a guardian, or a personality. In addition to creating a strong bond, this also prepares your talisman to receive your intention during the ritual given in chapter 11.

I recommend reading this meditation a few times before you try it so you become familiar with its flow. This will make it easier to guide yourself through it. You can also record yourself reading it aloud and play it back.

To begin, pick up your talisman and hold it gently in your left hand. Sit comfortably and, if you can, rest your feet flat on the floor. Close your eyes and feel the surface beneath you, the floor or chair that supports you. Take a nice, deep breath in, then slowly exhale. For the next few moments, focus softly on your breath and allow your body to relax.

Send your awareness to your talisman. Feel its weight in your hand. As you breathe in, draw its energy to you. As you breathe out, greet it and introduce yourself. Take a moment to connect as your breathing settles into a natural rhythm. As you inhale, invite the energy of your talisman into your hand. Let its energy flow through your hand, into your heart center, and then throughout your entire body. Feel the moving flow of energy. What does that energy feel like? Does it feel heavy or light? Vibrating or still? Do you see any colors or hear any sounds?

As you exhale, send your energy back into your talisman, letting it resonate with you and flow between you. As you continue to breathe, see if you can feel your energy coming into attunement with its energy. Visualize the pattern of an infinity symbol as you breathe in its energy and breathe your own energy back out to it. Visualize that symbol as the energy flows back and forth. What does the energy of your talisman feel like? What do you notice? Does it flow quickly or gently? Do you feel a vibration, or is it still? Do you hear anything? See anything? If not, don't worry. Just continue to breathe and trust that all is unfolding as it needs to.

If there is anything that you want to ask your talisman, now is the time. This can be a specific question, like how you can best work together, or a word, or a feeling. Send your message to your talisman and wait for a response. Again, don't worry if the answer isn't clear. Everything will be revealed in time.

Send gratitude to your talisman and, when you're ready, call your energy back to yourself. Release the connection to your talisman and breathe deeply as you open your eyes.

MUSINGS

- Write down anything you want to remember from the meditation, as well as any messages, impressions, or questions you want to explore further.

- How do you feel about your talisman now?

- Do you need to expand or adjust your intention based on this meditation?

In the next chapter, we'll discuss how to choose the most powerful time to conduct your talisman consecration ritual—the crucial step that transforms your talisman into a magical tool.

CHAPTER 9

Timing Your Rituals

I've always had a knack for timing, at least when it comes to small things. More often than not, when I listen to my intuition, I arrive at a restaurant or attraction just before a colossal waiting line forms. Or I get the last one of an item just before it sells out.

When it comes to the bigger things, I also see a pattern in my life of knowing when to make significant changes, when to leap into the unknown, or when to do something that others think is foolish. Somehow I just seem to know that it will turn out well and that, if I don't do it now, that option will no longer exist. This instinct has helped me get out of a job, or a city, or a situation while the getting was good.

That is why I suggest that, as you decide on the timing for your talisman ritual, you read through the suggestions in this chapter, but then listen to your own intuition. If you feel excited and eager, if your gut is telling you to strike while the iron is hot, do it. Don't wait for some far-off date in the future just because it may be more auspicious. And if your intuition tells you it's better to wait, pay attention.

The consecration ritual given in chapter 11 transforms a mundane object into a magical tool. But it's the timing of the ritual that contributes to making it a personal, powerful, and meaningful experience for you. When you consider the timing of your magical work, you engage the energy around you, tapping into a resource you don't have to create or orchestrate. It's already there in the atmosphere, waiting for you.

When you make magic, you weave energy, resources, and allies together. This doesn't have to be a complicated or unwieldy process. When you choose meaningful elements that fit together elegantly, your magic flows and takes on a life of its own. Your intention, the material you choose for your talisman, and the time you choose to consecrate it should all be significant to you and complement each other.

When you chose your talisman material, you focused first on finding an object that fit beautifully with your intention—let's say, rose quartz for love. But then you discovered that you could add other layers of meaning—perhaps working with a heart-shaped rose-quartz pendant set in sterling silver to honor the Divine Feminine. All these layers of meaning help to empower you as you work to manifest your intention regarding love.

And this layering principle applies to timing as well. You may consecrate your pendant on a Friday, because that day relates to the color pink and belongs to Venus and Freya, goddesses of love. If you consecrate it on a Friday that happens to fall on a new moon, you call in associations with new beginnings and planting the seeds of intentions. Or perhaps you choose a Friday that falls on a number that is lucky for you or on a date that has meaning for you.

Here's a personal example. I got married on Friday the 13th because, knock wood, it has always been an auspicious day for me. Our wedding was in June, by tradition a lucky month for weddings that is named after the Roman goddess of marriage, Juno. The date fell on a Full Moon, representing the culmination of growth and time in our relationship (more than twenty years ago now). But don't over-complicate this so much that you never find the perfect day. Just look for patterns and meaning, and consider combinations and synchronicities that can make your magic more powerful.

There are several factors you can consider as you choose the best day for consecrating your talisman—or for doing any magic, for that matter—the day of the week, the phase of the moon, days that have personal significance for you, and holidays, special events, and seasonal occurrences. And don't forget to consider *right now!* Now is always better than never.

Let's take a closer look at each of these factors and how they can influence how you work with your talisman.

DAYS OF THE WEEK

Each day of the week has magical correspondences that you can use to add power to your rituals. When consecrating your talisman, choose the day of the week that aligns best with your purpose, your theme, and your intention. This is an easy way to add another layer of meaning to your work. It also encourages you to plan your ritual and stick to your timing—and get that magical work done. In the descriptions below, I include the meanings of the tarot cards that relate to each day.

Sunday

The sun, the provider of light and life, presides over Sunday. As such, Sunday is an auspicious day for magic that encourages you to shine brightly and pursue goals and intentions focused on success, recognition of your talents, and advancement in your career. Like the happy child on the Sun tarot card, the sun encourages you to be open to receiving blessings and abundance; it invites you to bring joy into your life. Think of how it feels to turn your face up to the sun's golden light, to feel its warmth on your skin. This is the energy of Sunday. Sunday is the right day if you intend to amplify your confidence and increase your vitality or your ambition or your charisma. The colors associated with Sunday are gold and yellow; materials associated with this day are crystals like citrine, honey calcite, and pyrite, as well as the metal gold or a piece of sun-shaped jewelry.

Monday

The mysterious moon is associated with Monday, so this is a powerful day for intentions centered on trusting your intuition, increasing your psychic abilities, and doing shadow work. Monday is also related to the Divine Feminine, to themes of connection with your inner goddess, and to women's rites of passage. As the first day of the work week, Mondays often leave people feeling moody and blue, and this emotionally charged atmosphere supports introspection, the quest for self-knowledge, and understanding the next steps on your life path. The High Priestess and the Moon cards love Mondays, so if those archetypes of dreams, visions, and ancient wisdom resonate with you, consider working your magic on this day. Monday's colors are silver and white; talisman materials include crystals like moonstone and selenite, as well as the metal silver or a piece of moon-shaped jewelry.

Tuesday

Tuesday belongs to Mars, so its energy is fiery, ferocious, and intense. If you're gearing up for a challenge and need to take on a warrior role, this day activates courage and fires up ambition. Tuesday is an excellent choice if your intention involves achieving victory in a conflict, protecting yourself and your territory, or asserting your authority. This day's energy will inspire you to pursue your passions relentlessly. The mighty combination of the Emperor and the Tower cards relates to Mars and Tuesday. As a bold leader, the Emperor has the drive and discipline to maintain a solid empire, while the Tower brings down structures that are crumbling from within and liberates you from ego-centered behaviors. Red and orange are Tuesday's colors; crystals like carnelian, bloodstone, and fire agate work well as talisman materials, as does jewelry shaped like a crown or other symbols of leadership and authority. Tuesday's metals are iron and gold.

Wednesday

Wednesday is connected with the planet Mercury, so its energy is fast and lucky. Like the god Mercury/Hermes—the clever trickster, traveler, and divine messenger—Wednesdays support intentions related to skillful communication, quick financial gain, passing exams with flying colors, and general resourcefulness. This day has the energy of the Magician card, so it is a good day to dazzle others with your mesmerizing wit, to come out ahead in a gamble, and to have a great time stirring things up. Mercury/Hermes is an ingenious problem-solver who is excellent at getting out of sticky situations, so if you're in one, this is the day for your magic. Wednesday's color is green (you may also see orange and purple mentioned), so emerald, fluorite, or amethyst work well as talisman materials, as does jewelry shaped like wings, a caduceus, or the planetary sign for Mercury.

Thursday

Thursday is connected with the planet Jupiter, making this is a powerful day for magic focused on long-term prosperity and success, good health, and protection for home and family. It is a favorable day to sign contracts, enter into agreements, or win legal battles. We associate Thursday with the gods Thor and Jupiter/Zeus, all potent leaders with thunder and lightning at their disposal, so magic feeds your strength and power on this day. The Wheel of Fortune card takes precedence on Thursday, making it the luckiest day of the week. Thursday's colors are royal blue, purple, and green, so crystals like green aventurine, lapis lazuli, or amethyst are superb choices for your talisman, as are tin or an alloy of tin like pewter or bronze. A piece of jewelry shaped like an oak leaf or an acorn might please Thor, as well as symbols that evoke the wealth and abundance you desire—a dollar sign, a treasure chest, a tree, a cornucopia, or fruit, grain, or fish.

Friday

The planet and goddess Venus reign on Friday, making it all about love. The day takes its name from Freya, the Norse goddess of love and beauty. Friday is your best choice if you intend to invite love into your life, foster self-love, or deepen a current relationship. Friday's magic is luxurious and sensual. Get romantic; surround yourself with lush nature; put on sumptuous clothing; sink into pleasure. The day's color is pink; talisman materials include rose quartz, kunzite, copper, and rose gold. Charms shaped like a heart, a rose, or an apple evoke love and tender feelings. The Empress, with the symbol of Venus on her shield and her plush throne, claims Friday as her own.

Saturday

Saturday is associated with Saturn—both the planet and the scythe-bearing god of time and harvest—so this day has a somber atmosphere. Saturdays are for endings and banishing magic. If your intention involves ending a challenging situation, cutting unhealthy energetic ties, or protecting yourself from negative influences, Saturday is a powerful choice. Navigating grief, grounding, and karmic or ancestral healing are also themes that resonate with this day. The final card of the Major Arcana, the World, relates to Saturdays, as it heralds significant endings and successful transitions. The colors of the day are black and purple, so black tourmaline, obsidian, smokey quartz, and iolite are good crystal choices; charms shaped like an hourglass, a clock, or a scythe honor Saturn and the passage of time.

MUSINGS

- Which day of the week fits best with your magical intention?

- Does the material you chose for your talisman correspond well with any of the days of the week?

- If you have chosen to work with a day of the week for your magic, choose an actual calendar date and mark it down. What date did you select, and why?

∞∞

PHASES OF THE MOON

The moon is a powerful ally in all our magical work. Its energy pulls us like the tides, impacting us emotionally and physically. If you feel an affinity with the moon, it's beneficial and natural to flow with her cycles and make the most of that momentum and support when creating your talisman. As a bonus, you'll honor the moon and deepen your relationship with its energies as you work your talisman magic. Get outside, look up, and appreciate the moon. Those energies will work to enhance your magic.

Each phase of the moon is suited to a particular type of intention and magic. To decide which one suits you best, first consider whether the magic you're working with your talisman aims to increase or decrease, invite or banish, or bring something to fruition or an end.

Waxing Phases

The waxing phases of the moon support magical work focused on increasing abundance, inviting in blessings, and bringing things to fruition. The new moon occurs when the sun, earth, and moon are aligned, with the moon in the middle. The part of the moon illuminated by the sun doesn't face the earth at this time, so the moon is invisible to us. This is the first lunar phase and the beginning of the lunar cycle, making it ideal for magic involving new beginnings, setting intentions, taking first steps, and planting seeds you intend to nurture.

After the new moon, the light increases and the moon becomes brighter and more visible. The phase between the new moon and the Full Moon is called the waxing moon. Energy rises and increases during this lunar phase. Work with this phase if your talisman intention is to grow and expand something in your life, whether that is love, money, career success, or confidence—anything you want more of. As the moon grows in strength, so does your magic. The waxing moon can also provide an extra push or motivation to complete a project or reach a goal.

Full Moon

The Full Moon occurs when the sun and the moon are aligned on opposite sides of the earth. At this time, the moon's sunlit side faces the earth, so it appears fully bright and magnificently illuminated to us. This lunar phase adds light and power to any magical work. The Full Moon is a spectacle that captures our hearts and imaginations. We watch it slowly grow in intensity through the waxing phases, and we feel its energy rising. When the Full Moon appears in all its glory, we share in the triumph and appreciate the beauty of the process.

The Full Moon represents the culmination of intentions, efforts coming to fruition, and fully achieving your desire. Its luminosity reveals what is hidden or unclear, and invites you to shine at your full strength. The light of the Full Moon clears stagnant energy and charges you up, while adding power to divination and psychic practices. If your intention for your talisman involves completing a long journey, or wrapping up a project that's taken years to complete, or succeeding on a path of healing you've been following for some time, then this is a beautiful time to work your magic.

Waning Phases

The moon's waning phases support work focused on decreasing, banishing, or endings.

The waning moon falls in the period between the Full Moon and the new moon, when the illuminated surface of the moon decreases. After the intensity of the Full Moon, the waning moon invites introspection and retreating within to integrate what was revealed or achieved during the fullness of the moon. It has a gentle energy that asks you to rest and release what no longer serves.

With its downward, decreasing flow of energy, this lunar phase supports magic to help you release, repel, and banish situations and behaviors from your life. As the moon fades into darkness, let unwanted energies, thoughts, or patterns steadily diminish, so that you are ready for a fresh start with the new moon.

The Dark Moon marks the point at which the barely visible waning crescent disappears just before the new moon rises. This is the final phase of the lunar cycle, so it represents a pause and an ending. Take advantage of this time to rest, to practice self-care, to pull some tarot cards, and to look within. This isn't the best time to start something new; instead, release what no longer benefits you.

This lunar phase encourages you to reflect on your talisman intention and consider if you need to adjust, refocus, or expand it. But if your intention involves instigating a significant ending or banishing or binding a negative force in your life, consider working with this quiet and contemplative moon.

MUSINGS

- Do you feel a connection with the moon? What thoughts, feelings, or memories does the moon evoke for you?

- Which phase of the moon best fits your talisman intention? Waxing, full, or waning?

- Would you consider working with a moon phase for your talisman consecration ritual?

DAYS OF PERSONAL SIGNIFICANCE

Your talisman is personal—created by you and for you—so you may decide to choose a day that is significant to you for its consecration. This may be your birthday, an occasion that marks the start of a new year filled with possibilities and beginnings, with starting new patterns. Some milestone birthdays in particular spark introspection and change, adding motivation and purpose to your intention and your magic.

The anniversary of a life event or achievement can be another powerful choice. Think of a time when you did something that took courage, when you called on your faith in yourself and your determination to achieve something. Remind yourself of what you're capable of accomplishing and tap into that energy by consecrating your talisman on that date. You can tie that day into your current intention—for instance, by consecrating a talisman for advancing your business on the anniversary of the day you founded it. Or you can call on the energies of a day with happy memories—perhaps when you traveled to a dream destination, or gave a great talk or performance, or graduated from school, or achieved a long-term goal. Did you leave a bad situation or relationship, or quit a toxic job? Did you positively change your behavior to support your health and well-being? If so, you can choose that day to empower your magic.

Another approach is to choose a day that's numerically significant to you— like a day that falls on your lucky number. Look for dates with repeating numbers that may have positive connotations. For instance, if your lucky number is two, February 2 or 22 may call to you.

Some numbers are considered lucky in certain traditions and cultures, so tap into that shared energy if it resonates with you. But don't be afraid to choose numbers and dates that are favorable for you personally. Remember, your talisman is your *personal* magical ally.

MUSINGS

- Do you have a lucky day or number? If so, why is it lucky for you? Is this a good day to consecrate your talisman?

- Think of an occasion when you triumphed at something outside your comfort zone. What did that experience tell you about yourself?

- How do you feel about birthdays and anniversaries? Would one of those occasions inspire you in your talisman ritual?

Holidays, Events, and Seasonal Occurrences

You can tap into the collective energy of events or occasions that are widely celebrated across a number of traditions. For instance, many people set intentions or create resolutions on New Year's Day, with the idea that the first day of the year adds significance and motivation to their force of will, making it easier to achieve a goal, break a habit, or encourage a new behavior.

Think of a holiday or festival that has meaning for you and supports your intention. Although it may seem a bit corny, Valentine's Day represents love or self-love. Halloween supports divination, connecting with ancestors, and going deeply into shadow work. Earth Day honors our planet and living in a way that nurtures and protects it.

I love creating talismans on Leap Days because February 29 is a magical bonus day on which you can do something you usually wouldn't have the opportunity, courage, or trust in yourself to do. I called one talisman my "Leap of Faith Talisman," thus tapping into the energy of the tarot Fool.

You can also commemorate and make use of natural occurrences. The movement of the sun and astronomical events like solstices and equinoxes have fascinated human beings for thousands of years. These celestial phenomena herald the transition from one season to the next, and you can work with that energy of change and transformation in your ritual.

There are two equinoxes each year. In the Northern Hemisphere, the vernal (spring) equinox occurs around March 20, and the autumnal equinox occurs around September 22. This is reversed in the Southern Hemisphere. At that time, the sun is directly above the equator, which makes day and night equal in length. The equinoxes provide a moment of pause when light and darkness are in perfect balance before the seasons change to spring or autumn.

The solstices occur when the sun's path in the sky is the farthest north or south of the equator. The winter solstice, which happens in the Northern Hemisphere around December 21 or 22, is the shortest day and longest night of the year. The summer solstice, around June 20 or 21, is the longest day and the shortest night. June marks the start of summer; December marks the start of winter. Again, those seasons are reversed in the Southern Hemisphere. The summer solstice celebrates life, growth, and fertility, while acknowledging the inevitable shift into shorter days. The winter solstice welcomes the return of the sun and gives thanks for surviving the harshest time of the year.

The equinoxes and solstices are compelling points of change, but you can work with the energy of each season as well, tailoring your magical theme and intention to them. Spring heralds new beginnings and growth; in summer, everything flourishes and daily life is easier; autumn brings the harvest and preparation for cold days and long nights; winter invites rest and withdrawal, hibernation, and dreaming.

And remember, *now* is always better than never. Don't wait for all the forces, options, planets, and events to align before you act. If you're feeling momentum and have the time to act *right now*, do it! Don't let your magical work get lost in a maze of procrastination and planning. Work with the energy at your disposal in this moment. Consider the energy of the season you are in, any holidays or observances that are near, and the day of the week or moon phase it happens to be. Draw on the energy that is all around you. Adjust your intention to come into alignment with it and make the most of that ambient energy if it makes sense and stays true to what you want to manifest.

MUSINGS

- Is there a holiday that has significance for you and aligns with your talisman theme? What is it, and what does it mean to you?

- Does your intention fit the energy of one of the seasons? If so, which one?

- If you chose to work on a particular day, why did you choose that day?

And now, it's time to get your cards out! In the next chapter, we'll explore a tarot reading that will guide you to laser-sharp clarity about your intention, and add focus and power to your talisman magic.

CHAPTER 10

Reading for Clarity and Wisdom

Now that you have identified your preliminary intention and chosen and cleared your talisman, it's time to call on the tarot to fine-tune that intention and put your talisman to work. In this chapter, you'll learn a simple tarot reading that can help you gain crystal clarity on what you want to manifest, how you want to feel, and the actions you need to take to start on the path to achieving your goals.

The tarot reading below reveals your motivations, your hopes, and your apprehensions, and shows you how they impact what you believe is possible for you. It can show you possible challenges and available resources, and how to manage them so that your magical work is free from self-imposed blocks or limitations. In fact, acknowledging these limitations often lies at the heart of whether or not your magic succeeds, because if your inner critic is telling you that you're incapable of doing something or not worthy of the life you desire, you may be playing too small with your intention without realizing it.

As you already know, your intention needs to be something that you *believe*, on some level, that you can achieve. But there are two sides to that coin. It's not helpful to create an intention that is pure fantasy and lies outside the realm of possibility due to genuine logistical constraints. But it's not helpful to set an intention that falls short of what you truly want because you are battling with self-doubt or low self-esteem either. This tarot spread helps you form an intention that expresses a deep desire for change. All you have to do is approach the cards in a non-judgmental way, with curiosity and compassion, and let them reveal your truth. Read this spread as you would for a good friend—with honesty, love, and faith.

You can use the information, inspiration, and guidance you gain from this spread to transform your intention into a powerful affirmation that you can then program into your talisman as you consecrate it. As a result, your talisman will become a touchstone that reconnects you with your reading, the feelings it evoked, and the knowledge you discovered.

MUSINGS

- You will be reading this tarot spread for yourself. Do you find it challenging to read for yourself?

- If so, what do you need to be aware of when you lay out the cards? Can you stay curious, compassionate, and open?

Spread to Clarify Your Intention

Before you begin, revisit your intention and any notes you made as you read previous chapters, particularly those concerning the meditation and one-card reading in chapter 6. If you need a refresher on how to approach a tarot spread, take a quick look at chapter 5. To prepare, have your cards handy, light a candle, and center yourself with a couple of nice, deep breaths. I recommend reading through the explanation of the spread first to ensure you're comfortable with the card positions and what they represent. There is no need to memorize it. Just gently keep the spread's main themes and your intention in mind as you shuffle the cards.

Start by looking through your tarot deck with the cards face up and choosing the card that most closely resembles your goal or illustrates how you want to feel. This is called choosing a card "actively." Lay this card face up on the table. It will occupy the #1 position in your spread.

It may not be easy to narrow your choice down to just one card. If you get stuck, go through the deck and divide it into separate piles—one for "maybe" and one for "no." Then go through the "maybe" pile and eliminate cards until you have just one. Think back to your one-card reading in chapter 6 and ask yourself: "Would I choose that card for this position, or do I want to choose something completely different?" As you consider these questions, rely on what you know about the card's meaning. Pay close attention to the scene you see on the card and how it makes you feel. Can you see yourself in that card, living your dream? Take your time and put aside any preconceived ideas you may have; enjoy the possibilities.

Now shuffle the rest of the deck and leave the rest of the cards in the spread up to the universe. Draw cards #2 through #8 and lay them face up on the table. Before analyzing these cards one by one, allow yourself a flash of intuition and an emotional reaction to what you see. Don't worry about the tarot's traditional meanings or the spread positions; just notice how you feel. Make a note of any cards, symbols, or figures that jump out at you, and be open to any helpful messages. Then, work through the first eight cards, using the descriptions below to guide you.

- *Card #1* answers the question: What intention will I manifest?

- *Card #2* answers the question: How do I feel about my intention?

- *Card #3* answers the question: What am I excited and hopeful about?

- *Card #4* answers the question: What am I apprehensive about?

- *Card #5* answers the question: How can I expand my vision of what is possible?

- *Card #6* answers the question: What resources do I have to help me succeed?

- *Card #7* answers the question: What talents and gifts can I call upon to support me?

- *Card #8* answers the question: What challenges will I need to navigate?

The ninth card answers a question that you create for yourself. Ask yourself what you want or need to know, then formulate your question, pull the card, and lay it face up on the table.

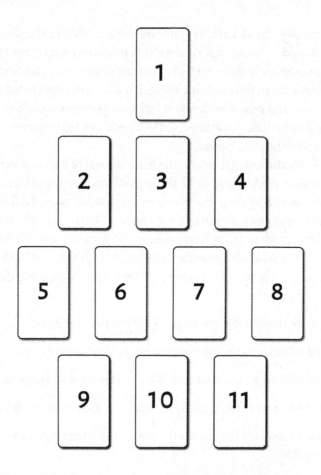

Finish by drawing cards #10 and #11 and laying them face up on the table. Interpret them using the descriptions below. At the end of this chapter, you'll find sample readings that show you how to combine these card meanings into a cohesive and impactful story.

- *Card #10* answers the question: What is the first step toward manifesting my intention?

- *Card #11* asks that you be given a card to inspire and guide you.

Now let's look more closely at what each of these positions represents.

Card #1: *What intention will I manifest?*

As you consider this first card, give yourself a moment to think about the intention that you want to manifest. You've already done substantial work in that direction; now go deeper and get more focused. Bring your intention to life. Your intention may be cut-and-dried, or measurable and practical, or more related to inner work or healing. Reflect on the general theme that came up for you in previous chapters, and ask yourself what you want to do, how you want to feel, and what you want to achieve. Jot down why you selected this card. Was it the general atmosphere of the card? Do you want to be the person on that card? Did the presence of a particular symbol seal the deal?

Card #2: *How do I feel about my intention?*

The card that shows up here may surprise you. It may reveal any fears that are holding you back from what you want to achieve. It may give you sharper insight into the changes and results you hope to manifest through your intention. Or it may show that you're excited and confident, and ready to move forward with your magic. Whichever of these is true, this card will take you deeper into your motivations. Notice if it is in alignment with the intention that you are in the process of setting. Does it express your feelings? Does it uncover hidden factors? Note down what you discover.

Card #3: *What am I excited and hopeful about?*

This card reminds you why you're setting this intention and doing this magic. It is meant to inspire you with possibilities and keep you motivated and on track. It may even show you a secret desire that you keep close to your heart. Go ahead and get excited; be hopeful. If this is a challenging card, sit with it and ask yourself where you see hope. Record the feelings that this card evokes for you.

Card #4: *What am I apprehensive about?*

This card presents a possible block or cause of hesitation that may keep you from achieving your goal. Sit with it; be honest with yourself. What scares you? What makes you nervous? What are you unsure about? Is it an external factor outside your control? Or is it an internal and personal challenge? Address the fear or apprehension in the card and look for clues that can help you understand, release, heal, or mitigate it. Write about this card freely; don't censor your thoughts. This is just for your eyes.

Card #5: How can I expand my vision of what is possible?
Card #5 helps you be aware of how you may be limiting yourself or downplaying what you believe is possible when you pursue your intention. When looking at the card, see if it is more expansive than what you're allowing yourself to dream. Maybe you've hit it just right and can leave it as it is. Maybe you get an inkling that you've created an intention that is so big that you don't believe it's possible. Whatever your impression, it is important to address what is going on with this card. Be playful and tap into what you want without self-doubt or judgment. When you're ready, jot down your thoughts. Do you need to expand or contract your intention? Or can you leave it as is?

Card #6: What resources do I have to help me succeed?
Resources are any helpers that you have at your disposal. You may already be aware of these assets, but chances are there is something that you've overlooked or dismissed. These allies can come in many forms—your talents, your experience, time, skills, finances, relationships, mentors, or loved ones. When you look at this card, ask yourself if you see an internal quality or an external resource on which you can rely for support. Make a note of anything you discover .

Card #7: What talents and gifts can I call upon to support me?
This card may show you talents that are specifically advantageous for your intention, or it may show you abilities you've undervalued or ignored. It may even show you talents of which you're well aware, and which you are now excited and ready to use. Identify at least one strength or skill you see on the card and note it in your journal—bonus points for more than one.

Card #8: What challenges will I need to navigate?
Identifying challenges needn't be daunting. This card can give you valuable information that will help you prepare for difficulties you're already anticipating and warn you of unforeseen circumstances, so you can head into your

manifestation magic armed with knowledge and confidence. As with other spread positions, this card can reveal challenges stemming from your mindset—your perspective, your emotional outlook, and your thought patterns. Or it may address external factors you can't control and have to accept, like the current state of the economy, world events, politics, and other people. In any case, look for the nature of the challenge and note any helpful advice the card presents. Make a mental note or record both in your journal.

Card #9: A question created by you.

Once you've examined the first eight cards and considered the information, insights, and gut feelings they provoked, pause and ask yourself: "What do I need or want to know now?" "What information is missing?" "Where do I want to take the story?"

A card in the spread that surprised or intrigued you may spark your question. Or you may formulate a question that is highly specific to your situation and intention, and not yet covered by the general spread. This spread position is your chance to ask the question in your heart, so make it personal and precise. Listen to your gut. The first question that comes to mind is usually the right one. Here are some ideas to get things flowing:

- What kind of healing do I need to achieve this goal?

- Who will help me on this journey?

- Is there a guide or ancestor who wants to work with me now?

- Is the timing I'm considering going to work?

- What is in my power to control?

- What is beyond my power to control?

- What's my superpower?

- What is the best way to approach this intention?

- How can I best support myself as I work with my talisman?

Card #10: What is the first step toward manifesting my intention?

Look for practical, concrete actions that you can take in this card. Stretch your-self to go beyond a vague idea and zero in on something you're going to *do* based on the card's image, its energy, or its meaning. This may be something you're excited about, or something you have been putting off. If it's the latter, trust that your effort will be worth the discomfort. Write down what you will do and, for a gold star, when you will do it.

Card #11: Give me a card to inspire and guide me!

Leave it open to the universe and let your guides show you what you need to see. Do you see yourself in the card? Do you see an ancestor, a guardian, or a loved one in the here and now? The image may depict you living your dream, or offer confirmation and encouragement, or advise you of a possible pitfall.

If you receive a challenging card, give yourself space to reflect on why it came up. There is a gift, or beneficial guidance, or an offer of support and heal-ing somewhere in that card, even if you don't recognize it immediately. Make a note of what inspires you about this card and the guidance it offers you.

What's Your Story?

Now that you have all your cards in front of you and you've made some notes about your initial impressions of each one, let the card positions fade into the background and look at your spread from a bird's-eye view. What story does it tell? What do you notice when you see all the cards together? Do any of the cards jump out at you? Do you notice any particular symbols? Any repeating symbols? Does one Minor Arcana suit dominate? Are they balanced? Are any suits missing? Do any Major Arcana cards make an appearance? How do the cards relate to each other? Do your cards look different from when you first laid them out? Make notes on your impressions and keep your spread in front of you as you create your affirmation.

Below, you'll learn how to create powerful affirmations that align with your intention and empower your magic. But first, let's look at some sample tarot readings that illustrate how to weave the card meanings and their positions into stories that can help you in your manifestation work.

SAMPLE READINGS

Below are four sample readings that illustrate how to weave the meanings and positions of the cards into a story that resonates for you.

Career Satisfaction and Financial Abundance

I did this reading for myself, leaving myself open to whatever the universe wanted to show me. My meditation had revealed that, although my work is rewarding and satisfying, I've let my career and life get out of balance. My body, mind, and spirit crave less stress, more faith in myself, and time to enjoy the abundant life I'm creating. The Nine of Pentacles, my one-card reading, supported these themes and pointed out that confidence, self-discipline, and ease are key factors in achieving my intention. I have included the affirmation that this spread inspired. Refer to the descriptions above and in previous chapters to refresh your memory about card meanings and positions.

Card #1: The World

I'm not aiming too high, just for the World! I chose this card because it represents the successful completion of a significant phase of life or a project, and the freedom and joy I can gain from it. I have many ideas and projects in progress, and I have the determination and stubbornness to keep working on them. But I draw things out longer than necessary when I don't have a deadline. My over-thinking and my perfectionist inner critic add anxiety and fear of failure to the mix. The World is my deadline, my intention to complete a project by a specific time and celebrate that victory. Then I can move up to the next level in my life, my career, and my personal development.

Card #2: The High Priestess

The High Priestess is my tarot "soul card," so I wasn't surprised to see her here. But I'm still grateful for this affirmation that I'm on the right path. I realize this intention is close to my heart and deeply connected with my identity. So rather than getting overwhelmed by it all, I can trust my intuition to guide me and enjoy the ebbs and flows of the experience. The High Priestess is *me* as a diviner, an introvert, and an empath. The project I'm working on flows from these parts of me. Not everyone will understand my choices along this path, and that's okay.

Card #3: King of Cups

I had to sit with this one for a while. The Kings don't usually come up for me, nor do they particularly resonate with me. I see this King's ability to weather all storms, rise above emotion, and flow smoothly toward the future, and that is something I am working on. Kings are established experts; the King of Cups is a kind advisor. I hope to reach this level of ease in my profession and as a mature adult. Cups relate to intuition, divination, and empathy, so this King shows my hope for mastery in these areas.

Card #4: Nine of Wands

The King of Cups and the Nine of Wands are facing off. The King, representing my hopes, is cool and collected, and larger than life; the Nine is wary. He's built a fence to protect himself and looks small and apprehensive. The Nine of Wands is determined and never gives up, but has been on high alert for too long and has forgotten how to shut down and relax. Perhaps I'm apprehensive about stepping forward, taking on more, and sharing my expertise. Burnout may have limited my capacity to take on new endeavors, so it's time to rest and replenish myself.

Card #5: Nine of Pentacles

This card came up in my one-card reading in chapter 6, so I was happy to see it here. And this Nine is in sharp contrast to the Nine of Wands—ease versus vigilance. My intention feels positive and achievable. This card encourages me to pursue the life of abundance, productivity, and enjoyment I desire. I don't need to expand on that vast World card I chose for Card #1. This card shows me that I can accomplish what I want if I move forward with consistency, effort, and confidence. It reminds me to enjoy the world I'm in right now, while dreaming of the one I want to create.

Card #6: Three of Swords

The Three of Swords is a visceral image. I see it as hard-won lessons, painful mistakes, and disappointments that bring knowledge. To achieve my intention,

I've got to regulate negative thought patterns that don't serve me well, and focus on lessons learned rather than ruminating on the past. The figure on the Nine of Pentacles looks back toward the Three of Swords and acknowledges it, but isn't consumed by it. My resilience is a resource that I can rely on.

Card #7: Queen of Cups

First the King of Cups, and now the Queen! I love the Queen of Cups and feel comfortable in this role. She is compassionate, a healer, and a great listener, and she offers empathy and sound advice. These talents and gifts will support me, and I can add the layer of pragmatism provided by the King of Cups.

The Queen asks me to revisit the King of Cups in position #3. What does that King truly mean to me? Am I hoping for more confidence or recognition of my expert status? By contrast, the Queen immerses herself in her emotions and intuition; she's more concerned with her healing work than she is with how other people perceive her. Do I want or need both roles?

Card #8: Knight of Swords

I've never been fond of this intense Knight, but I know the energy well. In the spread, he's charging at the Queen, bringing in the intrusion of the logical mind, while she floats gently in her emotions. I'll have to be careful not to be so laser-focused on small details that I lose sight of the bigger picture. Don't rush forward too fast; don't get lost in false urgency. I have to pace myself and remember to enjoy the journey rather than hurry through it.

Card #9: Nine of Cups

Three Nines came up in the spread, leading toward culmination, completion, and getting ready for change. The Nine of Cups is the "wish come true" card; success, contentment, and dreams are realized. My question was: "Am I following a path on which I can be successful and that will make me happy?" This card gives me a resounding "yes."

Card #10: Temperance

Temperance is a significant universal card, but a gentle one. On the higher level, the first step to manifesting my intention is to resolve any inner conflict around the project on which I'm working and find my flow. On a practical note, I will address my workflow and make an effective plan and schedule that support me. Work better, not harder.

Card #11: Two of Pentacles

The Two of Pentacles is a manageable, actionable, practical little card, and I see a connection to the World card in the repeated infinity symbols. The inspiring message is that I'll get there in the end if I adjust, be flexible, and learn the ropes along the way.

There is also a strong connection between Temperance and the Two of Pentacles. Look at the figures' poses; notice their feet and the pouring or juggling back and forth. If I find my flow in the practical aspects of life now, that will lead to more significant changes in my behavior patterns. As with the King of Cups, the same red ships are coming in.

What's My Story?
My spread included three nines, which indicate that I'm heading toward the end of one cycle and the beginning of another. This pattern tells me that I'm preparing for a transition, which will culminate in the World.

The High Priestess and Temperance cards are the only Major Arcana that came up on their own—I chose the World—and they share the themes of balance, wisdom, and quiet focus. All four suits of the Minor Arcana appear in the spread: Swords and Wands unsettle me, but Cups and Pentacles are comforting and abundant.

- *Talisman material:* A pyrite pendant set in sterling silver.

- *Keywords:* Freedom, success, wisdom, living my life purpose, mastery, confidence, determination, healing, self-worth, abundance, ease, experience, resilience, empathy, focus, trust, wishes come true, joy, balance, adaptability, finding my flow.

- *Affirmation:* I live a purposeful life, confidently pursuing my dreams and enjoying the abundance I create.

Transition into Retirement

This client, whom we met in chapter 6, is considering retirement and starting a new business venture and is wondering if the time is right. Her meditation confirmed that she is ready to say farewell to a rewarding but stressful career, which opens intriguing possibilities. Her one-card reading was the World, which also affirmed that she is ready for the transition into her next phase of

life. But it is imperative to her that she leave on her own terms, fulfilling her responsibilities and not leaving behind any loose ends. Her intention started to form: Achieve a smooth transition into retirement, with pride in her accomplishments and no regrets.

Card #1: Two of Wands

When actively choosing her first card, my client noticed that the figure on this card carries a globe, so it holds the World in its hand. This scene made her think of the World card in her one-card reading, but it felt more within her control and manageable. The wand attached to the wall represents her career and the solid legacy she leaves behind. By contrast, the wand the figure holds is an exciting new possibility—new horizons to ponder and ultimately to pursue.

Card #2: Knight of Cups

This card shows that she is about to embark on a romantic quest, following her heart and pursuing secret dreams she'd pushed aside over the years. She's well equipped for the adventure, with her shining armor and nimble horse; she's not feeling panic, but she's ready to get going.

Card #3: Eight of Cups

This card echoes the theme of the previous one. She is excited about leaving her comfort zone and heading into the unknown. It isn't easy to bring a long and meaningful career to a close, but she's restless. And melancholy intermingles with the desire for new experiences.

Card #4: Six of Cups

So far, this row of cards is made up entirely of the suit of Cups, and my client was surprised to see so much emotion surrounding her decision to retire. The Six of Cups evokes happy memories and nostalgia. It is a sweet and loving card. But here, it is coming up as a source of apprehension. She said that she would miss working with colleagues who had become good friends, and hoped that she'd be able to maintain those relationships. On another note, the Six of Cups is a cozy card that shows little action. She admitted she was concerned that she'd slip into complacency and inertia, rather than following new interests and passions.

Card #5: The Fool

This woman laughed out loud when she saw the Fool and took it to mean that she should leap foolishly into retirement without trying to plan everything ahead of time. Retirement is a leap of faith; it brings change and unknowns. But hesitating on the brink is no fun. She compared the Fool to the Two of Wands she selected to represent her intention, which depicted her as dignified and contemplative. The Fool brings in much-needed lightness and spontaneity.

Card #6: The Magician
The Magician lets her know that she has all the tools she needs to orchestrate a triumphant retirement and an engaging future. Her best resource is herself. She also realized that it is up to her to direct the course of her exit. If she doesn't act and make her intentions known, no one else will do that for her. In fact, she's so capable and admired that her colleagues would be happy to keep her in this role for years to come.

Card #7: Six of Wands
This woman is a born leader who can rally support around her when needed. She doesn't need to rest on her laurels, but it wouldn't hurt to remind people of everything she's accomplished. The acclaim and support of others will remind her of her talents and make the transition into retirement more joyful. She's already put her plans in motion and is excellent with follow-through, so she should keep riding the momentum and stay on course.

Card #8: Two of Cups
Like the Six of Cups, this Two depicts a sweet partnership and a concern. She saw herself and her spouse in this card, and the strength of their loving relationship. Yet she realized that the changes that she plans to make will significantly impact their lives. The Two of Cups suggested that open communication is crucial, and that some decisions are better made together.

Card #9: Ace of Cups
The Two of Cups weighed on her mind, so she asked for further information about how retirement could impact her relationship and how she could nurture and honor that partnership. The Ace of Cups appeared with a simple message of love. She mentioned that work had consumed both her and her partner over the past few years. And although they were happy, they'd been spending less and less quality time together. Now they would have an opportunity to refresh

and replenish their connection. Her intention to retire and start something new can also bring a fresh start for them as a couple. She can consider this transition a gift that opens possibilities, and approach it with compassion and gratitude.

Card #10: Eight of Pentacles
The main message from the Eight of Pentacles is to focus on what must be completed at work before she retires. She has a lot on her plate, so it's best to get down to it. She must be consistent and methodical, and get things done, while remembering that she's close to the finish line.

Card #11: Ten of Pentacles
In her eagerness to retire and free herself from the current burdens of her job, this client brushed aside the legacy she created with her work. The Ten of Pentacles asked her to pause and appreciate her body of work, the financial abundance she'd created, and how she'd been able to share her resources with family and loved ones. She will remember to celebrate the end of this chapter, and look forward to more additions to her legacy. She will continue to have a positive impact on the world.

What's Her Story?
The only two Major Arcana cards in this spread, the Fool and the Magician, make a powerful pair. The Fool has faith and potential, while the Magician manifests changes and opportunities.

The Knight and Eight of Cups and the Six of Wands are all moving in the same direction, heading toward the future. The Two of Wands and the Fool appear to be looking back. This woman's focus is on moving forward, but she appreciates the past and continues to learn from it. This spread is awash with Cups, so retirement may raise more emotion than she anticipates, and relationships with loved ones will play a vital role in her decision-making.

- *Talisman material:* A golden globe-shaped pendant.

- *Keywords:* New horizons, following dreams, unknown paths, friendship, happy memories, a leap of faith, spontaneity, magic, capability, victory, support system, love, fresh start, focus, work, completion, legacy.

- *Affirmation:* I'm excited about new adventures as I bring my current career to a satisfying conclusion.

Moving On from a Relationship

When we last saw this client in chapter 6, she was considering ending a romantic relationship, but hesitating because she still feels an attachment. She's invested years of time and energy in this relationship, yet she's increasingly unhappy. Her meditation opened feelings she had been pushing away—this relationship leaves her feeling unworthy and unloved, and she knows there is more for her. She isn't looking for a new romance; she just wants to move forward, to heal from what she's experienced, and to see what's next for her. The Ten of Swords came up in her one-card reading, indicating an inevitable and painful ending that brings relief, release, and a new dawn. Her intention started to form: End her relationship and focus on her own well-being.

Card #1: The Star
Although she appreciated the honesty and bluntness of the Ten of Swords in her one-card reading, this client chose the Star, a gentle and uplifting card, to represent her intention. She wanted to shift her focus away from the break-up and place it firmly on herself. The Star represents coming back to herself and fostering self-love and self-esteem. She wants to remember how to shine.

Card #2: Queen of Pentacles
Aside from her relationship, this person feels secure in other areas of her life. Her career is thriving; she takes care of her finances. Now she's ready to invest in herself and her well-being. She saw herself in the Queen of Pentacles and liked the independence, capability, and pragmatic wisdom that the Queen exudes. It gave her confidence to see herself in this way. Leaving a relationship isn't easy, but she knows she can make that break and manage the practical consequences.

Card #3: The Wheel of Fortune
The Wheel of Fortune spins, ushering in change and forward movement. This card reflects her hope for change and release from hesitation and indecision.

She doesn't mind that this card also brings the unknown and can't be controlled; she is excited about no longer feeling stuck. It also gives the impression that the timing is right for her to act, taking advantage of lucky opportunities and synchronicities as they appear.

Card #4: Seven of Swords

This woman is apprehensive about confrontations that may arise when she ends this relationship—with her partner, her family, or her friends—and wants to avoid them as much as possible. She knows she'll eventually face criticism and well-meaning advice, and she's afraid she will be perceived as self-serving and dishonest. She doesn't want to do herself a disservice by hiding or tiptoe-ing around what she must do, but she's anxious about the risks involved. The Seven of Swords advises her to look out for her interests, and shows her that she'll have to take risks to make the best of this tricky situation and find the most intelligent way out of it.

Card #5: The Empress

The Empress is an amplification of the Queen of Pentacles that appeared as card #2, confirming that this client's intention is on the right track, while encouraging her to expand her ideas to include a higher level of self-care, sov-ereignty, and self-love. The Empress lets her know she can create a life that feels as luscious, abundant, and satisfying as the image on the card. She should treat herself like an empress and expect respect and love just as she gives it. The first step is the healing indicated by the Star; then the Empress follows as she comes into her full power.

Card #6: The High Priestess

Her greatest resources in this context are internal—self-knowledge, wisdom, and intuition. Everything she learned over the past few years in her relation-ship is coming into play, and that valuable information will support her through this transition. The rolled-up scroll that the High Priestess holds reminds her of her daily journal, which helps her make sense of her thoughts. When she feels unsure, she re-reads her own words, which gives her confidence. Just as that journal is private, the High Priestess advises her to keep her thoughts and plans to herself. Privacy and boundaries are also fundamental resources.

Card #7: Ace of Cups

The Ace of Cups is a gorgeous card that shows a capacity for love and com-passion. Despite the deep pain she's experiencing now, this woman's heart never runs out of hope. She believes in love. This overflowing cup made her smile. Although she'd been feeling emotionally drained lately, it's good to see she can refill her own cup. She has the gift of seeing blessings and expressing gratitude during difficult times.

Card #8: Ace of Swords

The Ace of Swords is the second ace in the reading. The Ace of Cups is a gift of love and healing; the Ace of Swords offers a challenge. It will be challenging for her to stick to her decision and have unwavering conviction in herself and her judgment.

Card #9: Seven of Pentacles

At this point in the reading, this person understands that her mindset and internal factors are the primary drivers of her intention. Still, she is aware that break-ups are also surrounded by practical and logistical matters. So she asked the cards if there is anything she needs to do now to prepare for her separation from her partner in a pragmatic sense. When the Seven of Pentacles appeared, she realized the importance of looking at her finances and resources, and ensuring that everything is in order. The gardening tool on which the figure on the card leans shows that he is contemplating whether anything needs to be cut or pruned, telling her that it would be wise to cut any financial ties she has with her partner to avoid future entanglements.

Card #10: The Chariot

The charioteer wears impressive armor that is protective, but not heavy. He looks bold and triumphant. A few things came to mind with this card. My client had booked a solo vacation at a spiritual retreat center, but was considering canceling it because of the unsettled situation with her partner. The Chariot gave her the green light to *go*, and hinted that the experience would bolster her confidence and provide her with some shiny, metaphorical armor. On another level, the focus and clarity of the Chariot encouraged her to decide how she would leave this relationship, so that she'll no longer exhaust herself by pulling in different directions.

Card #11: Strength

The message we saw in this card was that, if this woman can handle a lion with such grace and poise, she can handle anything. Trust is the repeating message in the spread. Have faith in your capability and strength to manage and navigate any challenges that come your way. She also felt inspired by the calmness of Strength, which showed her that leaving this relationship doesn't have to be filled with drama and upheaval. By staying in a position of strength and being mindful of her reactions, she can achieve the peace and healing of the card she chose at the beginning of the reading—the Star.

What's Her Story?

Aside from the Star, which she chose, five Major Arcana cards appeared in this reading, showing the significance of the situation and how transformational it will be. The Wheel of Fortune and the Chariot show that there are some aspects of her life that she can control and direct, and some she can't. So how she reacts is important. The Empress, the High Priestess, and Strength are powerful Divine Feminine archetypes, reminding her of her wisdom, her fortitude, and her beauty.

Swords showed up as challenges; Cups and Pentacles appeared as gifts and resources; Wands were nowhere to be seen. Listening to her heart, her intuition, and her practical side will serve her well, but over-thinking and worrying will not. She should avoid passionate arguments and volatile tempers as well.

- *Talisman material:* A star-shaped fluorite crystal pendant wrapped in silver wire.

- *Keywords:* Hope, healing, security, luck, change, stealth, cleverness, self-love, sovereignty, intuition, wisdom, love, truth, decision time, confidence, ready for change, in the driver's seat, grace, compassion, strength.

- *Affirmation:* I navigate difficult situations with compassion and strength as I focus on my path forward.

Inviting Love into Your Life

When we met this client in chapter 6, she had been single for a long time and was ready to invite love into her life. Her intuition tells her the time is right; her heart is hopeful. Her eyes are open to unexpected possibilities that don't repeat old and disappointing romantic patterns. Her one-card reading, the Queen of Pentacles, advised her to nurture her well-being and finances, and find contentment in her own company before she embarks on a relationship. Her intention started to form: to invite a romantic relationship into her life, and form a partnership that would be a source of happiness, passion, and support.

Card #1: Queen of Pentacles
Since the Queen of Pentacles came up for her one-card reading, she decided to embrace it and get to know this practical and capable Queen better. She wanted to maintain the bright, secure, and satisfying life she'd already created on her own, and to know that, regardless of her relationship status, she's in a good place personally. This Queen's energy also supports her in attracting a romantic relationship that is nurturing, mature, and generous.

Card #2: Four of Wands
This card looks like a party! She is excited about the prospect of new love, and she has the support of friends and family who also want her to find a partner who makes her happy. When I mentioned that this scene could represent a wedding or an occasion worth celebrating, she said the idea of marriage or living with a committed partner is appealing to her now, whereas in the past, she had felt ambivalent or even opposed to it.

Card #3: The Sun
The child on the Sun card is beaming with delight, arms spread wide to receive all blessings. This woman said she feels that way, too. She's excited and hopeful about a relationship that gives her the room to shine with someone who appreciates her and celebrates her successes with her. She also wants to experience more joy and fun in her life, and is hopeful that a romantic relationship will contribute to that.

Card #4: The Fool

But she doesn't want to be made a fool of again. She said she tends to throw herself into relationships. Her common sense goes out the window, leaving her disappointed and hurt. She doesn't want to lose her spontaneity and willingness to take a leap of faith, but she's hoping to avoid wasting her time and energy on someone who isn't suitable for her.

Card #5: Three of Wands
The figure on this card is looking into the distance, to the far horizon. This suggests that this person can expand her search for a partner in a literal way; she doesn't have to stick to her immediate geographical area. This card also reminded her of someone she'd been interested in in the past, but she didn't pursue that connection because the logistics of a long-distance relationship daunted her. She thought she might reach out to that person now.

Card #6: Three of Pentacles
The Three of Pentacles suggests she might meet a potential romantic partner through her work—a colleague or a client. She travels regularly for her job, so this card tied in to the idea that the Three of Wands sparked—meeting some-one from farther afield. Professional relationships, networking, and mutual interests are resources for her to explore.

Card #7: Page of Pentacles
This woman doesn't want to play the Fool, but some Page energy will serve her well. Pages are curious and look at life, or love, with fresh eyes. The slow and steady Pentacles bring in practicality and a level head. Despite her appre-hension, she has a Page's openness and the Pentacle's willingness to nurture what is precious to her. She thought that a Page appeared as a gift or talent in her spread, rather than a King or a Queen. So allowing herself to be vulnera-ble and learn as she goes is a beneficial approach.

Card #8: The Emperor
She also saw herself in the Emperor. She's been on her own for a long time and realizes that the give-and-take that comes with a relationship may be chal-lenging—at least at first. But she much preferred the joyful openness of the Sun and the gentle self-confidence of the Page to the rigidity of the Emperor. On another note, she recognized an imperious ex-partner in the face of the Emperor, and challenged herself to let any attachments with that person go.

Card #9: Two of Cups

When this client asked the cards what kind of partner or relationship would suit her best at this time, she was happy to see the sweet and romantic Two of Cups. On noticing that the figures on the card were seeing eye to eye and standing on level ground, she knew that she needed a genuine heart connection with an equal partner who isn't afraid to share her hopes and fears and deepest feelings. Good chemistry wouldn't hurt, either.

Card #10: Ace of Wands

When she saw that magic wand in the Ace's hand, she knew that she had to act rather than wait for love to find her. She'd recently felt a spark of attraction with someone, and she decided to ask that person out and see where it led. Perhaps this person isn't her Two-of-Cups love, but she will only know if she takes that chance. She also found the idea of online dating intriguing and had been considering trying it as well.

Card #11: Ten of Cups

The Ten of Cups is the over-the-rainbow happily-ever-after card. Inspiring indeed! It looked to this woman as if the couple from the Two of Cups got to know each other and traveled a path that eventually led them to the domestic bliss of the Ten of Cups. She understood that it takes time and effort to establish a relationship like the one represented by this card, and that the journey to get there could be just as enriching as the culmination.

What's Her Story?

In the Fool, the Sun, and the Ten of Cups, the figures hold their arms open in wonder, spread wide to receive all blessings. This woman is ready to invite love into her life with the optimism, passion, and courtesy of the Pentacles, with common sense thrown in. The three passionate Wands and the three steady Pentacles balance each other, while the two Cups are overflowing with love and romance.

- *Talisman material:* Rose-quartz pendant set in sterling silver.
- *Keywords:* Sovereignty, well-being, practicality, celebration, joy, appreciation, foolishness, long distances, travel, networking, nurturing,

flexibility, connection, equal partners, heart to heart, magic wand, happily ever after.

- *Affirmation:* I attract a loving and supportive partner by loving myself.

AFFIRMATIONS

As you saw in earlier chapters, affirmations are positive, empowering statements you speak aloud regularly or say silently to yourself. By working with affirmations, you neutralize negative thought patterns that cause you stress, anxiety, and self-doubt, and replace them with an inner dialog that speaks to you with love and optimism. This fosters focus and self-esteem.

This inner dialog is a powerful force. It is always running through your mind, repeating the same things again and again. If you're not consciously aware of that voice, or if you're not consciously enabling it, you may be bombarding yourself with untrue, unkind, and useless stories that can keep you from achieving your goals. But when you work with affirmations, you empower that voice to deliver the messages you want to hear. This ensures that what you're telling yourself is beneficial and energizing, and moves you in the direction you desire.

Many people dismiss affirmations as ineffective or poke fun at those who use them. They think affirmations are just silly platitudes you use to tell yourself something that isn't true. They assume that those who use them are living in a fantasy world and asking a magical universe to send them whatever they want. And while it is true that telling yourself you are a millionaire doesn't make you one, it's especially true if you have no plan to become one and don't believe you ever will.

But this ignores the power that lies at the base of affirmations. Powerful affirmations are based on self-knowledge, courage, and determination. Like the intention you created for your talisman, they come from deep within and express a desire that you know will bring positive change to your life. By repeating an affirmation, you teach your brain that this statement is true and motivate yourself to behave in ways that help you manifest the desire expressed by your words. Effective affirmations *inspire you to action.*

Here are some important things you can do to ensure that the affirmations you create are powerful.

- *Create a strong intention:* Focus on one area of your life that needs love and care. Ask yourself what would make you happy and what kind of change you desire.

- *Frame your statement positively:* Don't invite negativity into the mix; it just breeds more. For example, avoid statements like: "I'll stop neglecting my health and ignoring my body." Instead, say: "I support my well-being with a healthy lifestyle and self-care practice."

- *Be specific:* Vague affirmations lack focus and clarity about the result you desire. Include timing in your affirmation if it makes sense. For example, don't say: "I will get a university degree." Instead, say: "I will graduate in spring 2026 with an honors degree in anthropology."

- *Use the present tense:* This tells you and the universe that what you're affirming is already true. The present tense expresses your conviction and trust in the outcome. Use definitive words like "I am" rather than "I want to" or "I will."

- *Use first-person pronouns:* Pronouns like "me," "I," and "my" personalize your affirmation and keep it firmly focused on you.

- *Include emotional words:* Words that express how you feel show that you're living your affirmation. For example: "I'm so happy to work at a company that appreciates my talent and dedication."

- *Make it about you:* Don't worry about how others perceive you. And don't try to become someone else. Keep it focused on *you*. For instance, avoid statements like: "My family will be proud of me when I succeed." Instead, say: "I take pride in my accomplishments."

- *Keep it short:* Create clear and concise statements that are easy to remember and repeat.

- *Make it real:* Write your affirmations down and speak them aloud, even if that's just in private. Stating your affirmation is the first step toward manifesting it.

- *Visualize success:* Imagine what your life will look like when you realize your intention. Experience it now; tell your brain to process those good feelings now.

- *Meet yourself where you are:* Acknowledge your feelings and challenges, and don't force yourself into a place of toxic positivity. Focus on manifesting your future, while acknowledging what's happening in your life and where you are *right now*.

Now, let's put all these steps into action.

CREATING POWERFUL AFFIRMATIONS

The reading you've done so far and all the magical work you've performed have given you the tools you need to create powerful affirmations that will transform your intention into the beating heart of your talisman. Now it's time to bask in the result.

Begin by taking a breath and centering yourself. Release any tension you are holding. Using the four sample tarot spreads above, lay out a spread that reflects your intention and consider the cards you see before you. Let yourself see the entire message the spread holds for you. Soak it in. What wisdom do you see there? What helpful information? Give yourself some time to enjoy the images on the cards. Notice how they support each other and weave together to tell your story. No pressure. No expectations. Just explore, discover, and notice.

With the theme of your intention in your mind, examine the cards one by one. What word or phrase immediately occurs to you when you look at each card? What is the essential aspect of it regarding the intention you want to manifest? Write down at least one keyword or phrase inspired by each card, and circle the ones that most accurately reflect your intention and your desire for change. (You can refer back to chapters 3 and 4 if you need to remind yourself of the keywords for each card.) Using those words, follow the steps above to formulate a positive, empowering affirmation that encapsulates the message you received from the cards.

When you're ready, write down your affirmation. Don't worry about it being perfect right away. Or ever, for that matter. Get the essence of it down quickly; you can always go back and adjust. Clarity and emotion are what matters here. You don't have to be a poet or produce a work of staggering beauty. Your affirmation just needs to feel authentic to *you*, using words that you're happy to repeat to yourself regularly. If you need some inspiration, refer back to the affirmations in chapters 3 and 4.

It's important to understand that your affirmation is already effective *by itself.* You can say it to yourself first thing in the morning, during the day, or before falling asleep. You can call those words to mind along with the experience of your tarot reading whenever you need a boost. Then you can lock this intention and affirmation into your talisman and continue to work with it until you reach your goal. In the next chapter, you'll learn how to create a personal and powerful ritual to consecrate your talisman, imbuing it with the power of your intention and your affirmation.

◇◇◇

MUSINGS

- Say your affirmation out loud to yourself several times a day. It doesn't have to be eloquent or perfect, but be sure you love it and that it expresses your intention honestly and meaningfully. Make it your own.

- Spend some time with card #1 in your spread—the one you actively chose. Journal about why you chose it. Leave it out where you can see it. Visualize yourself in the card, embody its central figure, or engage that figure in a conversation. Additional messages and information may come through. Note anything you receive in your journal.

◇◇◇

CHAPTER 11

Consecrating Your Talisman

You were likely inspired to pick up this book because you felt a need for positive change and a desire to manifest an outcome that will enrich your life. If that is so, you've been working magic from that very moment! Everything you've done since then has added to the spell you're crafting. You set an intention and thoughtfully chose an object to use as a talisman, then you read tarot for clarity and wisdom. The final step is to consecrate your talisman and start working with it.

When you consecrate an object, a place, or a person, you set it aside from the mundane world and dedicate it to a sacred purpose or specific use. A consecration ritual transforms the object, the place, or the person into something special and imbues it with spiritual meaning and divine energy.

Once churches, temples, shrines, synagogues, and other religious structures are consecrated, they are then used only for religious rites. When sacred sites in nature are consecrated, they become sanctuaries for spiritual practice. People who are consecrated to spiritual service devote their lives to serving a higher power. Magical tools and altars can also be consecrated to a specific ritual use. And when you consecrate your talisman to your intention, its purpose will be to manifest your desired outcome.

In this chapter, we'll first take a look at rituals in general—how to create one, what's usually included, and what makes everything flow together well. Then you'll learn how to create your own ritual that will consecrate your talisman to your intention. The most important part of this ritual is a visualization meditation, and you'll find an example of one at the end of the chapter.

I encourage you to make your consecration ritual your own. You can make it as simple as you like, perhaps just doing a visualization. Or you can make it elaborate and dramatic. Whatever suits you best. Just make sure that your ritual includes aspects that are meaningful and beautiful to *you*. You don't have to follow anyone else's formula, and you can't get it wrong. Creating a basic ritual framework that works for you allows you to conduct your consecration confidently, while leaving room to follow the lead of your emotions and intuition.

THE ELEMENTS OF RITUAL

A ritual is a series of actions and words performed in a fixed order to express a concept, meaning, or event symbolically. Much like the tarot, rituals are based on symbolism. They are often related to spiritual practice, religion, or tradition, and consist of ceremonies that connect participants with each other, with the Divine, or with nature. When our lives feel uncertain, chaotic, or overwhelming, rituals provide us with a sense of control and reassurance.

Rituals are fundamental to the human experience. We all participate in them to some degree, from formalized events like weddings or coming-of-age ceremonies to small rituals we create for ourselves—starting each day with a meditation, writing in a journal, going for a run, or drinking a cup of coffee in the backyard.

Rituals are conducted mindfully, with intention. When you perform a ritual, you focus your attention and honor the present moment, adding significance and meaning to every gesture and word. By doing so, you tell the universe that this time and its purpose are sacred.

Although all rituals are different, there are some elements that are common to them all.

- *A clear purpose:* Clarity is power. It is important to be clear about why you're performing a ritual. Be sure that your intention is unambiguous, that your affirmation expresses your intention implicitly, and that you know exactly what result you desire.

- *Lack of interruption:* Make sure that you won't be disturbed when you're conducting your ritual. Set that time aside as sacred. Turn off your phone, shut down social media, and tell family members or housemates not to interrupt you. Any feline or canine companions will likely want to join in the fun, so decide ahead of time if it's best to tuck yourself away or invite them in.

- *A dedicated place:* Create a serene environment for your ritual. Tidy your space or find a spot in nature that feels energized and powerful. Clear the space, and prepare yourself as well—perhaps taking a ritual bath before you begin, adding herbs, oils, flowers, or crystals that correspond to your intention. Or just take a few deep breaths, ground and center yourself, and visualize a bright, white light permeating your entire body.

- *An altar:* An altar is a focal point for spiritual practice, meditation, and prayer. The objects on your altar represent deities, elements, or energies you wish to honor and include in your devotions and magical work. Your altar should be personal and contain items that are a beautiful reflection of who you are, what you believe, and what you hold sacred. If you decide to set up an altar for your consecration ritual, as opposed to one you use for daily practice, add objects that correspond to your intention and remind you of your purpose. Try to include items that engage your senses—a fragrant flower, incense, a candle, a bell, fruit, or sweets. You can also place your talisman and the tarot card you chose for position #1 in your reading on your altar. Although building an altar is optional—all you really need for the ritual is yourself and your talisman—an altar reinforces your intention and energy. Besides, assembling one can be a lovely ritual in and of itself.

- *Sacred space:* You must create a container for your ritual and the energy you raise. By doing so, you invoke protective boundaries that keep out any unwanted or negative forces. You can do this by envisioning a circle of light around the space where you're performing your ritual. Or you can cast a circle of protection by starting in the east and walking around the circle three times clockwise. You can also use a wand or raise your hand while visualizing light flowing from your fingers and forming a circle.

- *Invocation:* An invocation calls upon your guides or guardians or the deity you honor. It can also call your ancestors, asking for their support and blessing for your magical work. When you speak an invocation, you invite the presence of the Divine and activate the divinity that resides within you. You can honor the four directions and their corresponding elements by calling them in and requesting their guidance. Because the elements are connected to the tarot's four suits, this adds another layer of meaning to your ritual.

- *Energy:* You can raise energy by singing, toning, chanting, listening to music, drumming, dancing, speaking, clapping, stomping, moving your body, meditating—whatever energizes you. Be playful and get excited about the positive change that's coming. Trust your intuition, and move into the next step when you feel invigorated and your vibration has reached the right level.

- *Visualization:* Visualization is an essential part of ritual. During visualization, you vividly imagine your desired result and experience it energetically. It will feel real, as if you've already manifested your intention, and that intention and that feeling will imbue your talisman with power that will support your manifestion magic in the physical world.

- *Grounding:* When your magic is complete, it is important to bring your awareness back to yourself and your physical body. Eat or drink something. Send any excess energy into the earth.

- *A closing:* Rituals are usually closed by sending gratitude to the deities, guardians, and guides you invoked at the beginning of the rite. Thank them for their support and presence, and say farewell. Thank and release the four directions or elements as well. Finally, open the circle you created by walking around it counterclockwise, or visualize the circle of light gently fading away.

Once you've created the framework for your consecration ritual using these elements, you are ready to use that framework to support your own talisman consecration ritual.

Since visualization is such an important part of these rituals, here's an all-purpose talisman visualization you can try to get a feeling for how it works. If it resonates with you, you can use it just as it is. If you want to tailor it to your intention or add meaningful elements, that's wonderful. In either case, I recommend familiarizing yourself with the visualization's flow so you can take yourself through it. Or you can record yourself reading it and play it back when you're ready to begin.

MUSINGS

- Is there an aspect of ritual that makes you feel uncomfortable? If so, why do you think that is?

- Do you prefer a short, sweet, simple ritual? Or does an elaborate or theatrical one appeal to you?

- Will you create an altar as part of your ritual? If so, what items will you include on it?

- Do you work with a particular deity that you want to invite into your ritual? Or spirit guides or ancestors?

TALISMAN CONSECRATION VISUALIZATION

Before you begin, place your talisman and card #1 from the tarot reading you did in chapter 10—the one you chose actively—in front of you. Take a moment to shift into a comfortable, seated position, then soften your eyes and allow your mind and body to relax. Take a deep breath and hold it briefly, then release. Repeat this, then settle into a pattern of breathing in slowly and exhaling even more slowly. Let go of any tension you may be holding in your body—especially in your shoulders, your neck, and your forehead. Just let it evaporate with each breath. Feel the solid earth beneath you. You are safe and secure in this moment.

As you breathe, cast your mind back to the tarot reading you did in the last chapter. Reflect on the information and the inspiration that came to you. Try to recall the spread in your mind. What do you remember most clearly? Which cards float into your mind first? How did you feel as you looked at them? What did they say to you? Remember all the resources you have to call upon, the strategies to help you navigate all challenges. Recall the inspiration and excitement you experienced.

When you are ready, rest your gaze on the first card in your spread—the one you chose to represent the intention you will manifest with your talisman. Place it in front of you or hold it at arm's length. What is your reaction to the card? Do you smile, or frown, or laugh? Or do you have a completely different reaction? Do you notice a particular symbol or color or figure on the card? Give yourself a moment to breathe and let your eyes roam gently over the card. Try to record everything that you see in your mind's eye. Give yourself a moment to breathe, and drink in everything you see and feel.

After a moment, place the card back down in front of you and pick up your talisman. Hold it in your hands. If you need to shift to get back into a comfortable position, do that. Take a nice deep breath and, when you're comfortable, let your eyes close. Let your breath fall into a natural rhythm—slow, easy, deep. Send your mind's eye to the talisman you are holding.

Greet your talisman; call out to it. Feel its energy. It may feel warm or cool; it may vibrate slightly; it may seem heavy or light. Whatever you feel is good. Just feel it. Focus on your talisman and your tarot card, and stay open to any messages they send you. Continue breathing in a natural rhythm—slow, easy, deep.

As you breathe, notice your surroundings getting a bit hazy. Everything in the room or space softens and fades. When things become clear again, you see that you are now standing in the landscape of your tarot card. Look around you. Stretch your vision and look off into the distance. What do you see? What do you feel? Is it cool? Warm? Is there a breeze, or is it still? Is there a fragrance in the air? Immerse yourself in your surroundings.

As you start to feel comfortable and welcome here, you notice another being materializing in your tarot landscape. As it slowly takes form, it asks to join you. If it feels right, say "yes." When the figure is fully visible, you see that it is one of the people, animals, plants, or symbols on the tarot card you chose to represent your intention. Who or what has joined you here?

You immediately feel very relaxed and comfortable with this figure. It feels like meeting an old friend. Take a moment to tell the figure about your dream, your goal, or the intention you want to manifest. Be as brief or as detailed as you want. Then share your affirmation with your tarot companion. The figure listens carefully and nods in agreement. You can feel the love and encouragement, and the support that is offered.

Ask your tarot companion for guidance. How can this being help you reach your dream or achieve your goal? Let your companion's wisdom infuse you with hope and determination. Don't worry if you don't understand what is said; it will become clear in time. And don't worry if you don't fully hear the message; it will reveal itself in time.

Thank your tarot companion for the guidance you received. The figure accepts your thanks and offers you a blessing, then gently fades away. You are alone again in your tarot landscape. You look around and notice something on the ground ahead of you. You approach it, lean in, and take a closer look.

It is a treasure chest, a jewelry box, or a box of any kind you can imagine. Whatever form it takes is the one that is just right for you. You feel a sense of anticipation and excitement, as if something extraordinary awaits in that box. With reverence, you open it. Your talisman rests gently inside. Beside it, there is a paper scroll. When you pick it up and unroll it, you see that your affirmation is written on it.

What does it look like? Does it look like an illuminated manuscript? A simple statement printed in a simple font? Is it beautifully handwritten or is it a messy scrawl? Are the letters large and bold, or tiny and precise? Take a moment to read the words silently to yourself. As you read, you see that your talisman starts to glow with a bright, white light. Send the essence of the message written on your scroll to your talisman.

When you do, you feel a resounding "*yes*" coming back to you from your talisman. You can sense your own energy as a sparkling light, and you see it swirl and merge with the energy of your talisman in a beautiful and joyful dance. You can feel that you have reached an agreement; you will support each other in achieving your goal and manifesting your intention. You know that whenever you wear or carry or work with your talisman, you can access this source of strength and joy.

When you're ready, carefully roll up the scroll and place it back in the box with your talisman, then close the box. You know that the scroll will be safe, and that you can access it at any time. Take a moment to breathe and send out gratitude for these gifts, and for all that lies ahead.

Knowing you have received the confirmation and support you need, you can now fully return to your body and the present moment. Wiggle your toes and fingers, gently move your head, and feel the floor beneath you. Release any excess energy from your hands and feet into the floor and send it back to the earth. Take a slow, deep breath in and exhale slowly.

When you are ready, open your eyes and look at your talisman. It is now your personal, magical tool. Know that you have the power to manifest your intention and that, anytime you need to, you can call on the energy of that talisman to support you.

Performing Your Consecration Ritual

And now it's time to bring all your magical work together and take the final step in creating your personal, powerful talisman. Take a moment to breathe and check in with your body, mind, and spirit. How do you feel? Remember, you can't get this wrong. You don't have to be perfect; trust in your magic and enjoy this experience.

Before you begin, gather your tools—your talisman, card #1 from your tarot reading, and your affirmation (either memorized or written down). Familiarize yourself with the framework of the ritual you created earlier in this chapter—especially the visualization—or have notes on hand if you need them. Set up your altar if you're using one. Make sure you have some food or drink on hand to ground yourself after the ritual. And wear comfortable clothes that allow you to breathe and move. When you are ready, activate your "Do not disturb" plan. Then follow the visualization above (or one you have created for yourself), building it around your own intention and your own carefully created talisman.

After the ritual, write down anything you want to remember about this experience. Take all the time you need to return fully to your body If your talisman is a piece of jewelry, put it on. Your talisman is now fully consecrated and you are ready to begin working magic, with its support.

MUSINGS

- Will you use the all-purpose visualization? Or will you create your own?

- Do you have everything you need to conduct your ritual?

- When you have completed the ritual, reflect on your experience.

CHAPTER 12

Working with Your Talisman

Because of the steps you've followed to create your talisman, you can trust that it is already working on your behalf. Nevertheless, don't forget that you are integral to the success of your magic. Your talisman is a physical reminder of your intention—why you set it in the first place and how satisfied you'll feel when you achieve it. *But you still have to do the work!* Your talisman amplifies your determination and commitment while attracting serendipitous opportunities that invite your action. The two of you are in this together, supporting each other. As you work with your talisman, this bond strengthens, and the results become more and more astonishing.

You can work with your talisman in many ways. In this chapter, I share some of my favorite methods. But as with all the steps you've taken so far, choose what works best for you and fits your time and energy levels. A simple practice performed with focus and feeling will be just as effective as an elaborately structured one. Working with your talisman doesn't have to be "work." Think of it as spending time with a loved one and nurturing a relationship that brings you satisfaction and joy.

Your Magical Mindset

Your mindset is such an essential part of manifestation magic. The following practices will help you sustain a state of optimism, empowerment, and confidence so you can believe and trust in your own success. I don't mean to say that your confidence may not be shaken at times or that you won't have difficult days; that's just human nature. But because your talisman carries your emotions and your desires, it will be a loyal companion as you navigate the ups and downs of your journey toward your goal. The methods I outline below can help you acknowledge and understand your feelings when you falter, and help you navigate back to clarity and focus.

Because of the bond you are forging, keeping your talisman close to you during the manifestation process is crucial. The easiest way to do this is simply to wear it. Its presence on your skin constantly reminds you of your intention and your power to achieve it. This also places your talisman within your aura and energy field, so it can share its properties with you. When you wear your talisman, imagine that it is a magnet or an antenna that draws what you desire to you. You chose your talisman material for good reasons; by wearing it, you connect with and tap into its qualities and superpowers.

If your talisman isn't a piece of jewelry or you're uncomfortable wearing it, you can enjoy the same benefits by carrying it with you. Just be sure to keep it close—perhaps in your pocket or bag—so you can access it easily. Don't relegate it to the depths of your backpack or the bottom of your purse; you have to be aware of its presence, and touch it or hold it in your hand throughout the day.

Here are some practical steps you can take to deepen the bond you are building with your talisman and bring its power into your magic.

- *Meditation and visualization:* In chapter 8, you learned how to meditate to attune with your talisman. In chapter 11, you saw how including a visualization in your consecration ritual can increase your talisman's power to manifest. And you can also use this type of guided meditation as an ongoing practice to "charge up" your talisman and deepen your relationship with it. Start your day with a brief meditation that connects you with your talisman and brings your energy into resonance with it. Visualize what your life will be like when you've achieved your intention. Go for a vivid experience; feel it in your bones as if it has already manifested. Visualize any actions you intend to take that day that will move you closer to success. This practice will empower you, and charge up your talisman as well.

- *Affirmation:* You've already learned how to craft powerful personal affirmations, and now you can put that knowledge to good use. When you put on your talisman or pop it in your pocket, say your affirmation to yourself, silently or aloud, at least three times. Look in the mirror while you do this—into your own eyes. If that makes you uncomfortable, just pause and take the time to repeat your affirmation with focus, presence, and complete faith. Repeating your affirmation in this ritualized way at least once a day is essential to manifesting your intention. After that, you can repeat it whenever you need a boost of energy and confidence.

- *Journaling:* Keeping a journal dedicated to your experiences working with your talisman helps you track and celebrate your progress. Make note of any synchronicities and opportunities that come your way and how you acted upon them. Consider how you are committing to act upon them. Then write down any thoughts or impressions you have as you work with your talisman. Remember, this journal is for your eyes only, so you can write about anything you like, in any way you like. Your journal is a place to acknowledge how you're feeling and track your energy levels. It can make you aware of how your hopes and fears are impacting your mindset, and clarify your view of your intention. Record any messages or signs you receive, dreams that stay with you long after waking, and anything else you want to remember. Make a regular habit of writing in your journal—either in the morning as you approach your day, or in the evening when you reflect on everything that transpired. Or both.

- *Care:* When you're not wearing or carrying your talisman, treat it well. Keep it in a safe place that honors it—on your altar, in a nice box or a bag on a tidy shelf, or in a personal, private space. Clean and polish it regularly. Keep its energy flowing using one of the clearing techniques discussed in chapter 2. You don't have to clear it completely or return it to a blank state. Just release any excess emotion or unwanted energy it may have absorbed from you or the environment and people around you.

- *Daily routine:* Bring these practices together into a supportive daily routine. For instance, start your day with a meditation or visualization that incorporates your affirmation. Write a few words in your journal about how you're feeling and any actions you will take toward manifesting your intention. Wear your talisman all day and, at the end of the day, revisit your journal and record any successes you had, any signs you received, and any questions you want to ponder.

- *Monthly routine:* If your intention is ongoing or long term, try basing your routine on the moon's phases. Remind yourself of your purpose and charge up your talisman during a new moon. Then make plans and act using the energies of a waxing moon. Record what has come to fruition by the time the moon is full, and let yourself reflect and rest during a waning moon. On the anniversary of your consecration ritual, re-enact it, celebrating your progress and expanding or adjusting your intention as desired.

Daily Meditation

Daily meditation is a gentle, personal, and potent way to work with your talisman. In the example below, I incorporate several techniques—bringing your energy into resonance with your talisman, speaking your affirmation, visualizing the successful manifestation of your goal, and any actions that you commit to taking at once. You can personalize this meditation in any way you wish.

Before beginning, put on your talisman or let it rest in your hand. Sit comfortably and allow your body to relax. Feel the surface beneath you and how it supports you. Take a nice, deep breath. Let the air fill your lungs and expand your belly, then exhale. Repeat. As you breathe, send your awareness around your body. If you notice any areas holding tension, invite them to let go and relax. Feel the weight of your talisman on your body or in your hand. As you breathe in, draw its energy to you. As you breathe out, send greetings to it. Take a moment to connect with your talisman as your breathing settles into a natural rhythm.

As you breathe in, invite the energy of your talisman into your hand. Let its energy flow through your hand, into your heart center, and then throughout your entire body. Feel the moving flow of this energy. With your next exhale, send your own energy back into your talisman, letting the two resonate and flow together. Continue to breathe in a slow, deep pattern. Feel your energy coming into resonance with the energy of your talisman. Visualize an infinity symbol as you breathe in your talisman's energy and breathe your own energy back into it. See that symbol as the energy flows back and forth.

When you are ready, share your affirmation with your talisman. Speak it aloud or silently three times, knowing it is already manifesting on an energetic level. Your talisman receives your words, your intention, and your desire, and affirms its role as your partner, your amplifier, and your guide. Then take your affirmation a step further. What does it mean to you? How will your life change when you manifest it? How will you feel?

Relax, breathe, and visualize what your life will be like when you manifest your intention. Create a vivid image, full of movement and color. Include as much detail as you can. Where are you? What are you doing? Who are you with? How do you feel? Take as much time as you need to visualize that outcome, breathing naturally and keeping your body relaxed.

Now bring your awareness to the present moment. What action will you take today to move you closer to realizing your dream? What opportunities will you pursue? What attitude will you embody? Take as much time as you need to visualize how you will approach the day ahead.

When you are ready, send gratitude and love to your talisman and invite its support and guidance. Then pull your energy back to yourself, into your body, into the room where you're seated. Take a slow deep breath and exhale, then open your eyes, feeling loved, inspired, and energized.

MUSINGS

- How will you work with your talisman?

- Would a structured daily practice work well for you? Why? Why not?

- If you don't use an altar, where will you keep your talisman when you're not wearing or carrying it?

- How are you feeling as you embark on manifesting your intention? Write in your journal to clear your mind and focus your energy.

Releasing Your Talisman

You've manifested your intention! First of all, celebrate! Now you need to decide what you will do with your talisman once you have sent it love and gratitude for its excellent work. Some say that once you have manifested your intention, you should thank your talisman and then destroy it. If it is made of something flammable, they say, burn it. Or break it or bury it. But honestly, I can't bring myself to do that in most cases.

Instead, I prefer to perform a ritual that expresses my gratitude and releases my talisman from its obligation. I never use a talisman for another purpose; I let it rest when it's done its work. In a sense, I "decommission" it. In that way, it becomes a beautiful piece of jewelry I can wear, or a keepsake that brings up fond memories rather than a magical talisman. You can also leave your talisman as an offering in nature or on your altar.

Of course, when you're ready to release your talisman, you must do it with respect, gratitude, and care. This object carried your energy and your dreams, and worked with you to create the positive change you desired. It helped you connect with the earth and with spirit, and guided you as you discovered new depths of strength and wisdom within yourself. So be sure to say farewell with grace.

Here's a ritual I use to release my own talismans from their magical obligations. You can use this yourself, or you can create one that aligns with your needs and your intention. As always, do what feels right for you. If you decide to create your own personal ritual, refer back to chapter 11 to review the elements of ritual. They apply here as well.

Start by clarifying your purpose. You are conducting this ritual to thank your talisman for its support in manifesting your goal and release it from its responsibility to you. Clear your space and yourself (see chapter 2). If you're setting up an altar, do that now (see chapter 11). Gather any tools that you'll be using, and place your talisman on your altar, or wear it or hold it.

When you're ready to begin, create sacred space. You can do this by envisioning a circle of light around the space where you perform your ritual or you can formally cast a circle (see chapter 11). Call in any guides, guardians, deities, or ancestors you want to have present, as well as the four directions. Raise energy by singing, chanting, clapping, dancing, or doing whatever leaves you feeling invigorated. Feel the joy of attaining your goal and enjoy the bond you and your talisman have shared.

When you are ready, sit comfortably and settle in for a meditation. Take a nice, deep breath in, and exhale slowly. Repeat. As you relax your body fully, send your awareness to your talisman. Feel its energy answering yours. Just breathe slowly for a few minutes and enjoy the experience of your energy coming into resonance with your talisman. Imagine that you can see the flow of light between the two of you—the easy way that your vibrations match and complement each other.

Think about the journey that led you to manifest your intention. Consider the highs and the lows you experienced, the challenges and the triumphs. Send those memories to your talisman. Send your love and your gratitude, and thank your magical companion for its support, wisdom, and miraculous help. Thank it for sending messages, signs, and synchronicities. Thank it for raising your energy when you felt unsure or depleted. Thank it for inspiring you to take meaningful action. Thank it for its role in manifesting the change you needed.

Ask your talisman if there is anything further that it wants to share with you. Pause and breathe until you receive your answer. It may come as a feeling, or an image, or in words. Don't worry if it isn't clear; just be open to receiving it.

Tell your talisman clearly that it is released from its obligation to you. It has fulfilled its purpose, and now is free to rest, replenish, and just be. Send that message with joy and appreciation.

When you are ready, say farewell and pull your energy back to yourself. Send any excess energy into the earth. Say thank you and farewell to any guides, guardians, or deities present, and release the four directions as well. Open your circle; watch its light gently fade away. Pick up your talisman, or take it off if you are wearing it, and put it away.

MUSINGS

- How did it feel to release your talisman?

- Is there anything you want to remember or express now that you've said your farewell? If so, write that in your journal.

- What will you do with your talisman now?

- Now that you've achieved this intention, what's next?

Conclusion: Journey's End?

Well, it's been quite a journey. You have successfully formed a magical intention, explored the messages contained in the tarot, created and consecrated a powerful talisman, and worked your manifestation magic using these tools. Congratulations! Now take a breath. Take a moment to rest. Place your hand on your heart, and thank yourself for your effort, your focus, and your faith. Your journey is over.

Or is it? More likely your journey is just beginning. More likely you have just begun down the path of manifestation magic, carrying with you two important companions—your talisman and your tarot deck. Use them well and wisely as you work to bring positive change and transformation into your life.

Thank you for making magic with me. May you manifest your intentions with ease, joy, and trust in yourself. The universe is cheering you on, and I am, too.

Acknowledgments

My heartfelt thanks go to the many people who supported me as I wrote this book and throughout the years of my tarot career.

Thank you to my husband, Matthew, for his unwavering love and support throughout all our adventures. Thanks for driving me to my first "tarot camp" and accompanying me to many conferences, even though you're not into divination. You are my Hermes, my tech support, my graphic designer, my photographer, and the best date for wine and pizza. Thank you for putting railroad spikes around our yard, for planting rosemary at our garden gate, and for not questioning when you found salt and cinnamon at our front door. You are my darling.

Thanks to my Mom for loving me so completely. Thanks for your courage and your joyful heart, and for teaching me the importance of seeing the good in everyone. You opened my eyes to so many ideas and spiritual possibilities and continue to surprise me.

Thanks to my sister, who is brilliant and magical, and the kindest person I know. She puts her heart into everything she does and creates positive change wherever she goes. Some of the happiest days of my life have been spent with her, visiting ancient shrines and temples, exploring crystal shops, and just enjoying each other's company. Although you are younger than I am, you will always be much wiser than I could ever be.

Thanks to my Dad for thinking that everything I do is amazing, interesting, and worthwhile. You made it possible for me to study what I love, to travel the world, and to get to know who I am. You are my rock, my north star, and my home. I miss you every day.

Thanks to Willow the cat, for being the sweetest writing companion and for sharing your cat magic with me.

Thanks to Rachel Pollack and Mary K. Greer for showing me how magical life can be. I am grateful that I had the chance to study with you. Thanks for sharing your wisdom, your humor, and your knowledge so generously.

Theresa Reed, thanks for your guidance, your kindness, and your faith in me. You are a tarot rock star. And Amy Lyons, thanks for supporting a nervous, fledgling author. I'm so happy to be working with you and everyone at Weiser.

I send much love and gratitude to Carrie Paris, Ethony Dawn, Melissa Cynova, Marilyn Shannon, Benebell Wen, Chris-Anne, Shelley Carter, Deirdre Norman, and so many other tarot friends who have encouraged and guided me over the years. And to my tarot circle and beautiful, luminous tarot clients. It has been an honor and a pleasure to read the cards for you, and I'm grateful for your insights, your support, and your love of the cards.

Thank you, universe, for everything.

About the Author

Lori Lytle provides mystical and practical guidance with tarot as Inner Goddess Tarot. She is an introvert, empath, nerd, solitary witch, High Priestess, Gemini, overthinker, and devotee of cats and cards. Lori is the co-creator of the Unifying Consciousness Tarot. She has been a featured presenter at international tarot conferences, including the Northwest Tarot Symposium in Portland, the Light and Love Tarot Reading Festival in Montreal, and the World Divination Association's first virtual online conference. She is also an instructor in Ethony's popular Tarot Summer School. Lori's current work focuses on creating magical talismans with the support of the tarot, as well as tarot practices that are designed specifically to feed the sensitive introvert soul. Find out more about Lori and read her blog at *innergoddesstarot.com*.

To Our Readers

Weiser Books, an imprint of Red Wheel/Weiser, publishes books across the entire spectrum of occult, esoteric, speculative, and New Age subjects. Our mission is to publish quality books that will make a difference in people's lives without advocating any one particular path or field of study. We value the integrity, originality, and depth of knowledge of our authors.

Our readers are our most important resource, and we appreciate your input, suggestions, and ideas about what you would like to see published.

Visit our website at *www.redwheelweiser.com*, where you can learn about our upcoming books and free downloads, and also find links to sign up for our newsletter and exclusive offers.

　　You can also contact us at *info@rwwbooks.com* or at

Red Wheel/Weiser, LLC
65 Parker Street, Suite 7
Newburyport, MA 01950